50% OFF FTCE Reading K-12 Test Prep Course!

Dear Customer,

We consider it an honor and a privilege that you chose our FTCE Reading K-12 Study Guide. As a way of showing our appreciation and to help us better serve you, we have partnered with Mometrix Test Preparation to offer you **50% off their online FTCE Reading K-12 Prep Course.** Many FTCE Reading K-12 courses are needlessly expensive and don't deliver enough value. With their course, you get access to the best FTCE Reading K-12 prep material, and **you only pay half price**.

Mometrix has structured their online course to perfectly complement your printed study guide. The FTCE Reading K-12 Test Prep Course contains **in-depth lessons** that cover all the most important topics, over **300 practice questions** to ensure you feel prepared, more than **300 flashcards** for studying on the go, and over **40 instructional videos**.

Online FTCE Reading K-12 Prep Course

Topics Covered:
Language Arts

- Research and Theories of Reading Processes
- Text Types and Structures
- Reading Assessment and Evaluation
- Learning Environments and Procedures that Support Reading
- Oral and Written Language Acquisition and Beginning Reading
- Phonics and Word Recognition
- Vocabulary Acquisition and Use
- Reading Fluency and Reading Comprehension
- Reading Program Development, Implementation, and Coordination

And More!

Course Features:

- FTCE Reading K-12 Study Guide
  - Get access to content from the best reviewed study guide available.
- Track Your Progress
  - Their customized course allows you to check off content you have studied or feel confident with.
- 3 Full-Length Practice Tests
  - With 300+ practice questions and lesson reviews, you can test yourself again and again to build confidence.
- FTCE Reading K-12 Flashcards
  - Their course includes a flashcard mode consisting of over 300 content cards to help you study.

To receive this discount, visit them at www.mometrix.com/university/ftcereading/ or simply scan this QR code with your smartphone. At the checkout page, enter the discount code: **TPBFTCER50**

If you have any questions or concerns, please contact Mometrix at support@mometrix.com.

Sincerely,

 in partnership with

FREE Test Taking Tips Video/DVD Offer

To better serve you, we created videos covering test taking tips that we want to give you for FREE. **These videos cover world-class tips that will help you succeed on your test.**

We just ask that you send us feedback about this product. Please let us know what you thought about it—whether good, bad, or indifferent.

To get your **FREE videos**, you can use the QR code below or email freevideos@studyguideteam.com with "Free Videos" in the subject line and the following information in the body of the email:

    a. The title of your product

    b. Your product rating on a scale of 1-5, with 5 being the highest

    c. Your feedback about the product

If you have any questions or concerns, please don't hesitate to contact us at info@studyguideteam.com.

Thank you!

FTCE Reading K-12 Study Guide
Test Prep and Practice Exam Questions Book
for the Florida Teacher Certification
[2nd Edition]

Lydia Morrison

Copyright © 2024 by TPB Publishing

All rights reserved. No part of this publication may be reproduced, distributed, or transmitted in any form or by any means, including photocopying, recording, or other electronic or mechanical methods, without the prior written permission of the publisher, except in the case of brief quotations embodied in critical reviews and certain other noncommercial uses permitted by copyright law.

Written and edited by TPB Publishing.

TPB Publishing is not associated with or endorsed by any official testing organization. TPB Publishing is a publisher of unofficial educational products. All test and organization names are trademarks of their respective owners. Content in this book is included for utilitarian purposes only and does not constitute an endorsement by TPB Publishing of any particular point of view.

Interested in buying more than 10 copies of our product? Contact us about bulk discounts:
bulkorders@studyguideteam.com

ISBN 13: 9781637759653

Table of Contents

Welcome 1

   FREE Videos/DVD OFFER 1

Quick Overview 2

Test-Taking Strategies 3

Introduction 7

Study Prep Plan for the FTCE Reading Test 9

Research and Theories of Reading Processes 13

   Evidence-Based Reading Research 13

   Theories of Reading Processes and Development 14

   Instructional Applications to Theories of Reading Processes 15

   Practice Quiz 17

   Answer Explanations 18

Text Types and Structures 19

   Text Features of Literary and Informational Texts 19

   Differentiating the Text Features and Formats of Various Texts 23

   Selecting Appropriate Texts to Reflect the Backgrounds of All Learners 26

   Print and Nonprint Texts for Instructional Use 27

   Selecting Complex, Grade-Appropriate Texts 29

   Practice Quiz 31

   Answer Explanations 32

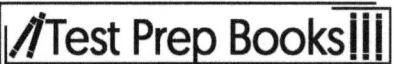

Reading Assessment and Evaluation 33

Screening, Diagnosis, Progress Monitoring, and Other Outcome Measures 33

Oral and Written Assessment Practices 34

Interpreting Student Data to Inform Small-Group Instruction 36

Interpreting Student Data to Inform Whole-Group Instruction 37

Using Data from Reading and Writing Assessments to Differentiate Instruction 38

Practice Quiz 44

Answer Explanations 45

Learning Environments 46

Grouping Practices 46

Speaking and Listening, Reading, Writing, and Viewing 46

Using Evidence-Based Practices to Motivate Learners 56

Incorporating Technology to Encourage Student-Centered Learning 57

Organizational Structures and Classroom Management Practices 59

Evidence-Based Intervention for Learners Who Have Not Mastered Grade-Level Standards 60

Practice Quiz 62

Answer Explanations 63

Oral and Written Language Acquisition 64

Oral Language Acquisition Concepts 64

Written Language Acquisition Concepts 66

Table of Contents

Practices for Developing Students' Reading and Writing Skills 67

Developing Narrative, Argumentative, and Expository Writing 69

Oral and Written Communication, Phonological Awareness, Print Concepts, Alphabet Knowledge, Decoding, Fluency, Vocabulary, and Comprehension 71

Practice Quiz 82

Answer Explanations 83

Phonological Awareness *84*

Phonological Awareness and Word Recognition Development 84

Developing Phonemic Awareness for All Learners 87

Phonics Knowledge and Decoding Skills 88

Word-Analysis Skills for Decoding and Encoding Words 93

High-Frequency, Sight, and Irregularly Spelled Words 97

Practice Quiz 98

Answer Explanations 99

Vocabulary Acquisition *100*

Vocabulary Acquisition and Use 100

Vocabulary Acquisition and Use in Speaking and Listening, Reading and Writing 102

Independent Word Learning Strategies 104

Conversational, Academic, and Domain-Specific Words 107

Practice Quiz 109

Answer Explanations 110

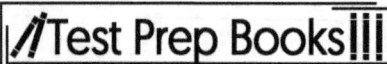

Reading Fluency and Comprehension *111*

Components of Reading Fluency that Support Comprehension 111

Developing Fluent Reading and Comprehension 114

Comprehension and Analysis of Informational Texts 115

Comprehension and Analysis of Literary Texts 116

Metacognition and Critical Thinking 118

Discussions of Literary and Informational Print and Nonprint Texts 121

Practice Quiz 123

Answer Explanations 124

Reading Program Development *125*

Involving Stakeholders, Including Caregivers, in Reading Initiatives 125

Reading Policies, Program Information, and Assessment Data 126

Comprehensive Reading and Reading Intervention Programs 128

Criteria to Determine the Effectiveness of Reading Programs 129

Improving Curriculum Content and Instruction 129

Collaborating with Others to Assist in Reading Instruction 130

Practice Quiz 133

Answer Explanations 134

Practice Test *135*

Answer Explanations *148*

Welcome

Dear Reader,

Welcome to your new Test Prep Books study guide! We are pleased that you chose us to help you prepare for your exam. There are many study options to choose from, and we appreciate you choosing us. Studying can be a daunting task, but we have designed a smart, effective study guide to help prepare you for what lies ahead.

Whether you're a parent helping your child learn and grow, a high school student working hard to get into your dream college, or a nursing student studying for a complex exam, we want to help give you the tools you need to succeed. We hope this study guide gives you the skills and the confidence to thrive, and we can't thank you enough for allowing us to be part of your journey.

In an effort to continue to improve our products, we welcome feedback from our customers. We look forward to hearing from you. Suggestions, success stories, and criticisms can all be communicated by emailing us at info@studyguideteam.com.

Sincerely,
Test Prep Books Team

FREE Videos/DVD OFFER

Doing well on your exam requires both knowing the test content and understanding how to use that knowledge to do well on the test. We offer completely FREE test taking tip videos. **These videos cover world-class tips that you can use to succeed on your test.**

To get your **FREE videos**, you can use the QR code below or email freevideos@studyguideteam.com with "Free Videos" in the subject line and the following information in the body of the email:

    a. The title of your product
    b. Your product rating on a scale of 1-5, with 5 being the highest
    c. Your feedback about the product

If you have any questions or concerns, please don't hesitate to contact us at info@studyguideteam.com.

Quick Overview

As you draw closer to taking your exam, effective preparation becomes more and more important. Thankfully, you have this study guide to help you get ready. Use this guide to help keep your studying on track and refer to it often.

This study guide contains several key sections that will help you be successful on your exam. The guide contains tips for what you should do the night before and the day of the test. Also included are test-taking tips. Knowing the right information is not always enough. Many well-prepared test takers struggle with exams. These tips will help equip you to accurately read, assess, and answer test questions.

A large part of the guide is devoted to showing you what content to expect on the exam and to helping you better understand that content. In this guide are practice test questions so that you can see how well you have grasped the content. Then, answer explanations are provided so that you can understand why you missed certain questions.

Don't try to cram the night before you take your exam. This is not a wise strategy for a few reasons. First, your retention of the information will be low. Your time would be better used by reviewing information you already know rather than trying to learn a lot of new information. Second, you will likely become stressed as you try to gain a large amount of knowledge in a short amount of time. Third, you will be depriving yourself of sleep. So be sure to go to bed at a reasonable time the night before. Being well-rested helps you focus and remain calm.

Be sure to eat a substantial breakfast the morning of the exam. If you are taking the exam in the afternoon, be sure to have a good lunch as well. Being hungry is distracting and can make it difficult to focus. You have hopefully spent lots of time preparing for the exam. Don't let an empty stomach get in the way of success!

When travelling to the testing center, leave earlier than needed. That way, you have a buffer in case you experience any delays. This will help you remain calm and will keep you from missing your appointment time at the testing center.

Be sure to pace yourself during the exam. Don't try to rush through the exam. There is no need to risk performing poorly on the exam just so you can leave the testing center early. Allow yourself to use all of the allotted time if needed.

Remain positive while taking the exam even if you feel like you are performing poorly. Thinking about the content you should have mastered will not help you perform better on the exam.

Once the exam is complete, take some time to relax. Even if you feel that you need to take the exam again, you will be well served by some down time before you begin studying again. It's often easier to convince yourself to study if you know that it will come with a reward!

Test-Taking Strategies

1. Predicting the Answer

When you feel confident in your preparation for a multiple-choice test, try predicting the answer before reading the answer choices. This is especially useful on questions that test objective factual knowledge. By predicting the answer before reading the available choices, you eliminate the possibility that you will be distracted or led astray by an incorrect answer choice. You will feel more confident in your selection if you read the question, predict the answer, and then find your prediction among the answer choices. After using this strategy, be sure to still read all of the answer choices carefully and completely. If you feel unprepared, you should not attempt to predict the answers. This would be a waste of time and an opportunity for your mind to wander in the wrong direction.

2. Reading the Whole Question

Too often, test takers scan a multiple-choice question, recognize a few familiar words, and immediately jump to the answer choices. Test authors are aware of this common impatience, and they will sometimes prey upon it. For instance, a test author might subtly turn the question into a negative, or he or she might redirect the focus of the question right at the end. The only way to avoid falling into these traps is to read the entirety of the question carefully before reading the answer choices.

3. Looking for Wrong Answers

Long and complicated multiple-choice questions can be intimidating. One way to simplify a difficult multiple-choice question is to eliminate all of the answer choices that are clearly wrong. In most sets of answers, there will be at least one selection that can be dismissed right away. If the test is administered on paper, the test taker could draw a line through it to indicate that it may be ignored; otherwise, the test taker will have to perform this operation mentally or on scratch paper. In either case, once the obviously incorrect answers have been eliminated, the remaining choices may be considered. Sometimes identifying the clearly wrong answers will give the test taker some information about the correct answer. For instance, if one of the remaining answer choices is a direct opposite of one of the eliminated answer choices, it may well be the correct answer. The opposite of obviously wrong is obviously right! Of course, this is not always the case. Some answers are obviously incorrect simply because they are irrelevant to the question being asked. Still, identifying and eliminating some incorrect answer choices is a good way to simplify a multiple-choice question.

4. Don't Overanalyze

Anxious test takers often overanalyze questions. When you are nervous, your brain will often run wild, causing you to make associations and discover clues that don't actually exist. If you feel that this may be a problem for you, do whatever you can to slow down during the test. Try taking a deep breath or counting to ten. As you read and consider the question, restrict yourself to the particular words used by the author. Avoid thought tangents about what the author *really* meant, or what he or she was *trying* to say. The only things that matter on a multiple-choice test are the words that are actually in the question. You must avoid reading too much into a multiple-choice question, or supposing that the writer meant something other than what he or she wrote.

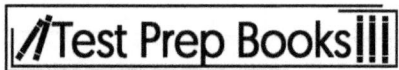

Test-Taking Strategies

5. No Need for Panic

It is wise to learn as many strategies as possible before taking a multiple-choice test, but it is likely that you will come across a few questions for which you simply don't know the answer. In this situation, avoid panicking. Because most multiple-choice tests include dozens of questions, the relative value of a single wrong answer is small. As much as possible, you should compartmentalize each question on a multiple-choice test. In other words, you should not allow your feelings about one question to affect your success on the others. When you find a question that you either don't understand or don't know how to answer, just take a deep breath and do your best. Read the entire question slowly and carefully. Try rephrasing the question a couple of different ways. Then, read all of the answer choices carefully. After eliminating obviously wrong answers, make a selection and move on to the next question.

6. Confusing Answer Choices

When working on a difficult multiple-choice question, there may be a tendency to focus on the answer choices that are the easiest to understand. Many people, whether consciously or not, gravitate to the answer choices that require the least concentration, knowledge, and memory. This is a mistake. When you come across an answer choice that is confusing, you should give it extra attention. A question might be confusing because you do not know the subject matter to which it refers. If this is the case, don't

eliminate the answer before you have affirmatively settled on another. When you come across an answer choice of this type, set it aside as you look at the remaining choices. If you can confidently assert that one of the other choices is correct, you can leave the confusing answer aside. Otherwise, you will need to take a moment to try to better understand the confusing answer choice. Rephrasing is one way to tease out the sense of a confusing answer choice.

7. Your First Instinct

Many people struggle with multiple-choice tests because they overthink the questions. If you have studied sufficiently for the test, you should be prepared to trust your first instinct once you have carefully and completely read the question and all of the answer choices. There is a great deal of research suggesting that the mind can come to the correct conclusion very quickly once it has obtained all of the relevant information. At times, it may seem to you as if your intuition is working faster even than your reasoning mind. This may in fact be true. The knowledge you obtain while studying may be retrieved from your subconscious before you have a chance to work out the associations that support it. Verify your instinct by working out the reasons that it should be trusted.

8. Key Words

Many test takers struggle with multiple-choice questions because they have poor reading comprehension skills. Quickly reading and understanding a multiple-choice question requires a mixture of skill and experience. To help with this, try jotting down a few key words and phrases on a piece of scrap paper. Doing this concentrates the process of reading and forces the mind to weigh the relative importance of the question's parts. In selecting words and phrases to write down, the test taker thinks about the question more deeply and carefully. This is especially true for multiple-choice questions that are preceded by a long prompt.

9. Subtle Negatives

One of the oldest tricks in the multiple-choice test writer's book is to subtly reverse the meaning of a question with a word like *not* or *except*. If you are not paying attention to each word in the question, you can easily be led astray by this trick. For instance, a common question format is, "Which of the following is...?" Obviously, if the question instead is, "Which of the following is not...?," then the answer will be quite different. Even worse, the test makers are aware of the potential for this mistake and will include one answer choice that would be correct if the question were not negated or reversed. A test taker who misses the reversal will find what he or she believes to be a correct answer and will be so confident that he or she will fail to reread the question and discover the original error. The only way to avoid this is to practice a wide variety of multiple-choice questions and to pay close attention to each and every word.

10. Reading Every Answer Choice

It may seem obvious, but you should always read every one of the answer choices! Too many test takers fall into the habit of scanning the question and assuming that they understand the question because they recognize a few key words. From there, they pick the first answer choice that answers the question they believe they have read. Test takers who read all of the answer choices might discover that one of the latter answer choices is actually *more* correct. Moreover, reading all of the answer choices can remind you of facts related to the question that can help you arrive at the correct answer. Sometimes, a misstatement or incorrect detail in one of the latter answer choices will trigger your memory of the subject and will enable you to find the right answer. Failing to read all of the answer choices is like not reading all of the items on a restaurant menu: you might miss out on the perfect choice.

11. Spot the Hedges

One of the keys to success on multiple-choice tests is paying close attention to every word. This is never truer than with words like *almost*, *most*, *some*, and *sometimes*. These words are called "hedges" because they indicate that a statement is not totally true or not true in every place and time. An absolute statement will contain no hedges, but in many subjects, the answers are not always straightforward or absolute. There are always exceptions to the rules in these subjects. For this reason,  you should favor those multiple-choice questions that contain hedging language. The presence of qualifying words indicates that the author is taking special care with his or her words, which is certainly important when composing the right answer. After all, there are many ways to be wrong, but there is only one way to be right! For this reason, it is wise to avoid answers that are absolute when taking a multiple-choice test. An absolute answer is one that says things are either all one way or all another. They often include words like *every*, *always*, *best*, and *never*. If you are taking a multiple-choice test in a subject that doesn't lend itself to absolute answers, be on your guard if you see any of these words.

12. Long Answers

In many subject areas, the answers are not simple. As already mentioned, the right answer often requires hedges. Another common feature of the answers to a complex or subjective question are qualifying clauses, which are groups of words that subtly modify the meaning of the sentence. If the question or answer choice describes a rule to which there are exceptions or the subject matter is complicated, ambiguous, or confusing, the correct answer will require many words in order to be expressed clearly and accurately. In essence, you should not be deterred by answer choices that seem excessively long. Oftentimes, the author of the text will not be able to write the correct answer without offering some qualifications and modifications. Your job is to read the answer choices thoroughly and completely and to select the one that most accurately and precisely answers the question.

13. Restating to Understand

Sometimes, a question on a multiple-choice test is difficult not because of what it asks but because of how it is written. If this is the case, restate the question or answer choice in different words. This process serves a couple of important purposes. First, it forces you to concentrate on the core of the question. In order to rephrase the question accurately, you have to understand it well. Rephrasing the question will concentrate your mind on the key words and ideas. Second, it will present the information to your mind in a fresh way. This process may trigger your memory and render some useful scrap of information picked up while studying.

14. True Statements

Sometimes an answer choice will be true in itself, but it does not answer the question. This is one of the main reasons why it is essential to read the question carefully and completely before proceeding to the answer choices. Too often, test takers skip ahead to the answer choices and look for true statements. Having found one of these, they are content to select it without reference to the question above. The savvy test taker will always read the entire question before turning to the answer choices. Then, having settled on a correct answer choice, he or she will refer to the original question and ensure that the selected answer is relevant. The mistake of choosing a correct-but-irrelevant answer choice is especially common on questions related to specific pieces of objective knowledge.

15. No Patterns

One of the more dangerous ideas that circulates about multiple-choice tests is that the correct answers tend to fall into patterns. These erroneous ideas range from a belief that B and C are the most common right answers, to the idea that an unprepared test-taker should answer "A-B-A-C-A-D-A-B-A." It cannot be emphasized enough that pattern-seeking of this type is exactly the WRONG way to approach a multiple-choice test. To begin with, it is highly unlikely that the test maker will plot the correct answers according to some predetermined pattern. The questions are scrambled and delivered in a random order. Furthermore, even if the test maker was following a pattern in the assignation of correct answers, there is no reason why the test taker would know which pattern he or she was using. Any attempt to discern a pattern in the answer choices is a waste of time and a distraction from the real work of taking the test. A test taker would be much better served by extra preparation before the test than by reliance on a pattern in the answers.

Introduction

Function of the Test

The Florida Teacher Certification Examination (FTCE) is the exam Florida teachers take in order to alleviate certification requirements for teaching. This guide explores the FTCE Reading grades K–12. A passing score on the FTCE Reading K–12 is one of several steps in becoming a certified teacher. This guide is for individuals who wish to become certified in teaching Reading K–12.

Test Administration

Computer-based tests for the FTCE are located in Florida as well as throughout the United States. Teachers are directed to visit the Pearson VUE website in order to find a testing center near them. They may schedule their appointment date while registering for the exam. Appointment dates are available year-round by appointment. Those who do not pass the test have to wait thirty-one days to retake it. Those who receive a passing score for the exam must wait three years to retake the test, if they still are not satisfied with their score. There are no limits to how many times a person can retest. Individuals with a documented disability may receive special accommodations, such as extra test time.

Test Format

When a person arrives at the testing center, they must bring two valid forms of ID. If an individual brings a sweater or overshirt, it must be checked by the testing center. Those who remove the sweater or overshirt in their exam room must place it over the back of the chair. Jackets and coats are not allowed in the testing room.

The Reading K–12 exam is a computer-based test (CBT) with 80 multiple-choice questions. The exam length is two hours and thirty minutes. Below are the sections of the FTCE Reading K–12 and their percentage of questions on the test.

Section	Percentage
Knowledge of research and theories of reading processes	10%
Knowledge of text types and structures	10%
Knowledge of reading assessment and evaluation	11%
Knowledge of learning environments and procedures that support reading	10%
Knowledge of oral and written language acquisition and reading and writing development	12%
Knowledge of phonological awareness, phonics, and word recognition based on the science of reading	12%

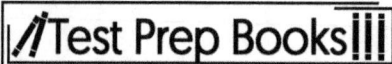

Section	Percentage
Knowledge of vocabulary acquisition and use based on the science of reading	12%
Knowledge of reading fluency and reading comprehension based on the science of reading	13%
Knowledge of reading program development, implementation, and coordination	10%

Scoring

Individuals must obtain a scaled score of at least 200 to pass the test. A decision of pass or non-pass is usually provided after completing the exam, unless an exam is being revised. Official score reports are available within four weeks.

In order to pass the entire exam, all subtests must be passed. Some may choose to send their scores to the Institution or Professional Development Certification Program (PDCP) during the registration process. A score verification process is also available, wherein test takers who did not pass the exam can review the multiple-choice questions they answered incorrectly.

Study Prep Plan for the FTCE Reading Test

1 **Schedule** - Use one of our study schedules below or come up with one of your own.

2 **Relax** - Test anxiety can hurt even the best students. There are many ways to reduce stress. Find the one that works best for you.

3 **Execute** - Once you have a good plan in place, be sure to stick to it.

One Week Study Schedule

Day 1	Research and Theories of Reading Processes
Day 2	Reading Assessment and Evaluation
Day 3	Incorporating Technology to Encourage…
Day 4	Phonological Awareness
Day 5	Reading Fluency and Comprehension
Day 6	Practice Test
Day 7	Take Your Exam!

Two Week Study Schedule

Day 1	Research and Theories of Reading Processes	Day 8	Word-Analysis Skills for Decoding and Encoding…
Day 2	Differentiating the Text Features and Formats…	Day 9	Vocabulary Acquisition
Day 3	Reading Assessment and Evaluation	Day 10	Reading Fluency and Comprehension
Day 4	Learning Environments	Day 11	Reading Program Development
Day 5	Incorporating Technology…	Day 12	Practice Test
Day 6	Oral and Written Communication…	Day 13	Answer Explanations
Day 7	Phonological Awareness	Day 14	Take Your Exam!

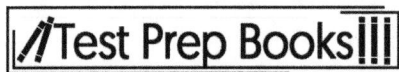

Study Prep Plan for the FTCE Reading Test

One Month Study Schedule

Day 1	Research and Theories of Reading Processes	Day 11	Evidence-Based Intervention...	Day 21	Vocabulary Acquisition
Day 2	Text Types and Structures	Day 12	Oral and Written Language Acquisition	Day 22	Independent Word Learning Strategies
Day 3	Differentiating the Text Features...	Day 13	Practices for Developing Students'...	Day 23	Reading Fluency and Comprehension
Day 4	Selecting Complex, Grade-Appropriate...	Day 14	Oral and Written Communication...	Day 24	Comprehension and Analysis of Literary Texts
Day 5	Reading Assessment and Evaluation	Day 15	Spelling as a Developmental Process	Day 25	Discussions of Literary and Informational...
Day 6	Interpreting Student Data to...	Day 16	Recognizing Common Orthographic Patterns	Day 26	Reading Program Development
Day 7	Response to Intervention (RTI)...	Day 17	Phonological Awareness	Day 27	Criteria to Determine the Effectiveness of Reading...
Day 8	Learning Environments	Day 18	Developing Phonemic Awareness for All...	Day 28	Practice Test
Day 9	Methods of Feedback in the Writing Process	Day 19	Word-Analysis Skills for Decoding...	Day 29	Answer Explanations
Day 10	Incorporating Technology...	Day 20	High-Frequency, Sight...	Day 30	Take Your Exam!

Build your own prep plan by visiting:

testprepbooks.com/prep

As you study for your test, we'd like to take the opportunity to remind you that you are capable of great things! With the right tools and dedication, you truly can do anything you set your mind to. The fact that you are holding this book right now shows how committed you are. In case no one has told you lately, you've got this! Our intention behind including this coloring page is to give you the chance to take some time to engage your creative side when you need a little brain-break from studying. As a company, we want to encourage people like you to achieve their dreams by providing good quality study materials for the tests and certifications that improve careers and change lives. As individuals, many of us have taken such tests in our careers, and we know how challenging this process can be. While we can't come alongside you and cheer you on personally, we can offer you the space to recall your purpose, reconnect with your passion, and refresh your brain through an artistic practice. We wish you every success, and happy studying!

Research and Theories of Reading Processes

Evidence-Based Reading Research

Valid Sources for Research on Reading

While teachers have access to an ever-increasing volume of sources, not every source is reliable. Some research is biased and presents facts that are not necessarily true; other sources are not researched at all and are based purely on personal experience. Teachers need to evaluate their sources for credibility before using them in the classroom, particularly when using material from the internet.

Here are some helpful questions you can ask yourself to determine whether a source is credible.

- Is the source published by a reputable organization? If you are not sure, research the publisher and make sure that it is trustworthy. Some examples of reputable sources are research journals, academic presses, and well-known organizations (such as libraries or museums). If you are conducting research online, you will find that these sources typically have web addresses that end with .edu or .gov. Some research journals are especially reliable because they have been **peer reviewed**, which means that they have been vetted by a team of experts before publication. Sources that are not reliable include personal blogs and social media posts: online, these sources will usually be on websites ending with .com.

- Who is the author, and what are their credentials? The best advice comes from experienced researchers and professionals. Information about personal experience, such as a post on a teaching blog, may help teachers brainstorm new ideas, but it is not as reliable as source material for research.

- Does the source use evidence to back its claims? Good research is grounded in fact, not speculation.

- What is the date of the source? Research is always advancing, so older sources are typically not as reliable as newer ones.

- Is the source's writing of a high quality? Numerous grammar mistakes, typos, and other errors indicate that the author or organization is not credible.

- Is the source unbiased? This question is particularly important when evaluating the findings from studies. For example, consider a study on the risks and benefits of teaching reading with computers and tablets. If this study is conducted by a major electronics company, it is not unbiased: the researchers have a considerable stake in the findings, and they may design a study that favors computer use.

Theories of Reading Processes and Development

Theories of Reading

There are three basic approaches to the reading process: bottom-up, top-down, and interactive.

Bottom-Up Approach

The **bottom-up approach,** sometimes called data-driven or text-based reading, views reading as a decoding process. This approach relies on behavioral psychology and conditioning; the child is exposed to a stimulus (the letter), and the child learns to react with the appropriate response (the sound). Essentially, the bottom-up approach breaks language down into its smallest unit: the **phoneme**, or individual sound (for instance, the word "think" contains four phonemes: /th/, /ee/, /ng/, and /k/). Children are taught to read through **phonics**, which is the relationship between letters and sounds. For example, phonics teaches children that the letter "b" makes the sound /b/. After learning the individual letters, they can **decode** text by putting the letters together to form words. This model was predominant in the 1960s–1970s.

Top-Down Approach

The **top-down approach** suggests that reading is a matter of guesswork rather than decoding. Readers begin predicting the content of a text by looking at its title, images, and surrounding context; as they read on, they test and refine those predictions until they understand what the text means. This theory is grounded in **Lev Vygotsky's social constructivist theory**, which states that children learn information by interacting with their environment as whole, not breaking it down into parts. The top-down approach focuses on **whole language** reading, in which children learn to recognize words or phrases as a whole instead of analyzing their phonemes. Words that a child recognizes without reference to their phonemes are called **sight words**. Sight words are usually short terms that appear often in the English language, such as "it" and "or." Top-down reading was favored in the 1970s–1980s.

Interactive Approach

The **interactive approach** attempts to integrate the first two approaches. It argues that bottom-up and top-down understanding occur simultaneously during the reading process; children can certainly decode by using phonics, but they also rely on contextual information and make predictions about the material. This theory advocates a balanced approach to reading, suggesting that teachers use aspects of both phonics and whole language reading in their curriculum. Some children will be stronger in one approach and some in the other; by uniting the two approaches, teachers can ensure that all their students succeed. This model gained traction in the 1980s, and it is still popular today.

Jean Piaget's Four Stages of Cognitive Development

Reading research also regularly refers to developmental theories. The most common of these theories is **Jean Piaget's four stages of cognitive development**, which are outlined below.

Sensorimotor Stage: Age Birth to Two Years

In the **sensorimotor stage**, children experience the world primarily through their senses. They explore the world through trial and error, manipulating the objects around them and trying to elicit a response. During this stage, children learn to coordinate their sensory experiences with motor responses. They also begin to build an understanding of language, but their skills are limited to cataloguing objects and making demands. The major development that takes place in this stage is object permanence. **Object permanence** is a child's ability to understand that an object continues to exist even if they cannot see it.

Preoperational Stage: Age Two to Seven Years

During the **preoperational stage**, children learn **symbolic thought**, which is the ability to see that one thing stands for another. For example, a child pretending that a stick is a sword is using simple symbolic thought; a poet using darkness to symbolize evil is using a more complex symbol. While sensorimotor children can only understand words that refer to concrete objects or actions (like "car" and "give"), preoperational children can grasp immaterial concepts like "difference" and "opposite." While children in this stage develop imagination and memory skills, they rely on intuitive intelligence rather than logic. They are **egocentric**, which means that they are focused on their own internal lives and struggle to relate to others. They also begin to understand **conservation**, which is the idea that a substance can change in appearance without changing in quantity. For example, pouring a glass of water from a tall thin glass to a squat glass does not change the amount of water.

Concrete Operational Stage: Age Seven to Eleven Years

In the **concrete operational stage**, children learn to form logical arguments. While most still cannot understand abstract ideas, concrete operational children learn to manipulate symbols more effectively, organize their thoughts into logical sequences, and grasp cause and effect relationships. They also become less egocentric: they understand that not everyone shares their experiences, and begin to make an effort to understand other people's thoughts and feelings.

Formal Operational Stage: Age Eleven Plus Years

In the **formal operational stage**, children progress to the highest level of symbolic thought: understanding abstract concepts. They learn to think about abstract ideas like "freedom" and "mercy," and can understand that the x in algebra stands for an unspecified number. They also begin to use **theoretical thought**, or "what if" scenarios like "if humans could upload their consciousness into machines, would these machines be human?"

Instructional Applications to Theories of Reading Processes

Applying Reading Theories in the Classroom

While most contemporary teachers use the interactive approach to teach reading, it is important to understand which model each teaching method stems from. Essentially, techniques that focus on the sounds of letters (phonics) rely on the bottom-up approach, while strategies that use sight words and guesswork are grounded in the top-down model. Each approach has its strengths and weaknesses. Purely phonetic readers can learn new words by themselves, but sometimes they read slowly because they sound out common words like "if." On the other hand, students who rely solely on sight words can read words they know quickly, but they cannot sound out new words and struggle to differentiate words that look similar. By using techniques from both approaches, teachers can ensure that their students draw from the strengths of both models.

Relating Piaget's stages of cognitive development to reading instruction is also helpful. Children typically learn to read in the preoperational stage. Since they are rapidly expanding their understanding of language in this stage, it is a great time to introduce new vocabulary words and help them learn to describe immaterial concepts. However, when picking reading materials, remember that these children are not ready for theoretical ideas and vocabulary. As children age and move into the concrete operational stage, they are developing empathy: hence, it is a prime time to introduce them to literature from a variety of perspectives, like multicultural literature. These children have also begun to form logical arguments, so discussion, presentations, and essays become valuable teaching tools. Finally, in the formal operational stage, children learn to grasp complicated ideas and words. They should learn to read and write articulately on more abstract and theoretical topics, like ethical issues and scientific theories.

Practice Quiz

1. A teacher using a word wall is most likely using which reading theory to teach their students?
    a. Interactive
    b. Bottom-up
    c. Top-down
    d. Decoding

2. Self-teaching, in which a student takes new content and reads and learns on their own, is less likely to be indicative of a student who learned to read via which reading theory?
    a. Top-down
    b. Interactive
    c. Bottom-up
    d. Decoding

3. A child capable of defining and understanding abstract words such as *love* is in which of Piaget's stages of cognitive development?
    a. Concrete operational
    b. Sensorimotor
    c. Formal operational
    d. Preoperational

4. Students who grasp the meaning of conservation understand which of the following?
    a. That symbols are used to economize language in writing and literature
    b. How to organize their thoughts into a logical sequence
    c. That focusing on themselves and their struggles requires energy
    d. That even though a substance can change the way it looks, that doesn't necessarily change the quantity

See answers on the next page.

Answer Explanations

1. C: The top-down method looks at reading holistically and suggests that it is more about guesswork than decoding. As a result, it relies fairly heavily on sight words, which are reinforced through tools such as word walls. Choice A is incorrect because the interactive strategy incorporates both top-down and bottom-up strategies. The bottom-up method suggests decoding is the best strategy; viewing whole words isn't part of that method, so Choice B is incorrect. Decoding, Choice D, is also part of the bottom-up strategy and is therefore incorrect

2. A: The top-down method focuses on whole words, so it typically takes longer for students to read and learn independently because they have not learned the decoding skills the other two theories include. Choice B is incorrect because the interactive method would have included strategies such as phonics in addition to sight reading, and therefore students taught via that method would have some of the skills needed to self-teach. The bottom-up theory focuses on breaking down words using phonics and phonemic awareness; a student taught this method will be able to decode words more quickly than those taught based on the top-down method, so Choice C is incorrect. Choice D is incorrect because decoding is the skill students learn through the bottom-up method; it is not a method, but a strategy of that method.

3. C: It isn't until the formal operational stage that students have a firm enough grasp of abstract ideas such as love to be able to define and understand the concept. The concrete operational stage, Choice A, is defined by a child's grasp of logic and awareness of others. Children in the sensorimotor stage, Choice B, are capable of understanding the concrete, or things that can be experienced through the senses. Therefore, abstract ideas, which cannot be experienced through the senses, would be difficult in that stage. Choice D, the preoperational stage, is defined by understanding concrete symbols, such as the way a stick can become a sword during imaginary play.

4. D: Students are learning to understand the concept of conservation. Although a container may hold five hundred gumballs, pouring them into a wider, flatter container still means there are five hundred gumballs. Choice A is incorrect because symbols have nothing to do with conservation. Organizing thoughts into a logical sequence, Choice B, doesn't appear until the next stage of development, so it is incorrect. Choice C is incorrect as well; although children in this preoperational stage are egocentric and learning conservation, their egocentrism isn't about conserving energy.

Text Types and Structures

Text Features of Literary and Informational Texts

Informational, Descriptive, and Persuasive Materials

It is important for students to be exposed to a variety of texts, reading materials, and resources. To become well-rounded readers, teachers should provide students with expository texts in addition to the classroom textbooks. Key characteristics of informational and expository texts include informative facts about a specific topic. Since these are nonfiction texts, diagrams or other graphic aids may be used to assist in understanding the text. Other forms of informational text include news articles, research journals, educational magazines with informational text, and websites. These texts can be used in small groups or can be introduced in whole group instruction, and then further explored in small intervention groups. Intervention groups are useful because they allow small groups of students to focus more intently on a particular problem, area of instruction, or topic than can be achieved by the group as a whole. They can be used both to address particular issues experienced by readers who are less fluent and to allow more advanced students to explore a particular topic of interest in greater depth.

Fact-based understanding and the use of textual evidence is imperative in expository and informational texts. Students should be able to compare and contrast two different texts and identify problems and solutions as well as cause and effect. Graphic organizers arranged chronologically can help students take notes when covering nonfiction texts. Students need to have the correct order of events in a nonfiction piece in order to identify the cause of an event, as well as the effect it had on problems and solutions. At times, students may need to compare and contrast two texts to identify the similarity of facts, the differences in reported facts, or note any bias from the author. Using knowledge of writing standards and instruction can aid students' understanding of informational text. When comprehending an informative text's objective, students should utilize their prior knowledge of the topic, prior writing assignments, and concluding sentences in the text. This is another example of how reading comprehension and writing go hand-in-hand in the learning process, and how writing and language become important to student comprehension.

Reading Comprehension Strategies

Organizational/Explanatory Features
Using and understanding references is imperative in developing reading comprehension skills. Pre-teaching a lesson on understanding references can be helpful, or a teacher may even incorporate this skill into teaching some broader comprehension skills. Prior to teaching from the basal reader, or prior to each story in the basal reader, a teacher should address the table of contents at the beginning of the textbook. This teaches students to use the table of contents frequently and allows them to find parts of a story that they will be reading on their own. When teaching from nonfiction texts, such as social studies or science, instruction should be provided on using the index to identify and locate specific information to answer comprehension questions. Both nonfiction and fiction texts can be used to teach how to use the glossary to locate boldfaced and important vocabulary. It is often most beneficial to identify and teach new vocabulary prior to reading a piece, so that students gain a deeper understanding of the text as they read it for the first time.

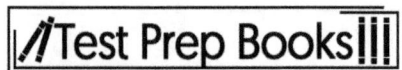

Text Types and Structures

Typographic Features

Understanding changes in the appearance of text will help students easily identify important information. Pointing out boldfaced words during reading instruction tells students these may be important words in the understanding of the text, and that new vocabulary may be present. Boldfacing or italics may help students identify when a thought or topic is changing or being brought to attention. Color-coding may be used when comparing or contrasting different parts of the text. During reading comprehension instruction time, it is important to point out when these changes occur. It is also helpful to try to find text of this nature to use in small group or whole group instruction. Text with these types of typographic features assist students on their path to reading comprehension.

Graphic Features

Graphics always help interpret a story or text. Younger learners rely on pictures to help tell the story, while older students use diagrams, maps, and charts to aid in understanding texts. Even for adults, graphic features assist with visualizing the text. Charts and diagrams help organize information into clear and concise patterns. Maps help understand specific places and locations. Illustrations help visualize a fictional story. Furthermore, illustrations with captions help visualize nonfiction and fiction texts, particularly when paired with captions that provide an explanation of why the illustration is important.

Main Ideas, Supporting Details, and Author's Purpose

Topics and main ideas are critical parts of any writing. The **topic** is the subject matter of the piece, and it is a broader, more general term. The **main idea** is what the writer wants to say about that topic. The topic can be expressed in a word or two, but the main idea should be a complete thought.

The topic and main idea are usually easy to recognize in nonfiction writing. An author will likely identify the topic immediately in the first sentence of a passage or essay. The main idea is also typically presented in the introductory paragraph of an essay. In a single passage, the main idea may be identified in the first or the last sentence, but will likely be directly stated and easily recognized by the reader. Because it is not always stated immediately in a passage, it's important to carefully read the entire passage to identify the main idea.

Readers should also remember that when most authors write, they want to make a point or send a message. This point or message of a text is known as the **theme**. Authors may state themes explicitly, like in *Aesop's Fables*. More often, especially in modern literature, readers must infer the theme based on text details. Usually after carefully reading and analyzing an entire text, the theme emerges. Typically, the longer the piece, the more themes the reader will encounter, though often one theme dominates the rest, as evidenced by the author's purposeful revisiting of it throughout the passage.

The main idea should not be confused with the thesis statement. A **thesis statement** is a clear statement of the writer's specific stance, and can often be found in the introduction of a nonfiction piece. The main idea is more of an overview of the entire piece, while the thesis is a specific sentence found in that piece.

In order to illustrate the main idea, a writer will use **supporting details** in a passage. These details can provide evidence or examples to help make a point. Supporting details are most commonly found in nonfiction pieces that seek to inform or persuade the reader.

A reader should carefully examine the author's supporting details to be sure they are credible. The reader needs to consider whether the supporting details provide evidence of the author's point and whether they directly support the main idea. Readers might find that an author has used a shocking statistic to grab their attention, but if the statistic doesn't support the main idea, it isn't effectively used in the piece.

Logical Organization and Structural Patterns in Nonfiction Text

Structural Patterns of a Text

Teaching students text structure helps them to search for information when answering questions about the text. This again integrates reading and writing strategies when learning about comprehension. Text needs should be written in a logical way. Consistent and logical written thoughts aid in comprehension and help readers find information easier within the text, especially when trying to locate answers to comprehension questions. Students should recall that the broader meaning of text is located at the beginning of a story, and more specific details are provided throughout the text. Subtitles will help students locate information they are seeking.

Local Organization

Nonfiction is inherently different from fiction, both in context and structure. Students will find that nonfiction lacks the metaphors, similes, and artistic structures of poetry or literature that are used to deliver symbolic meaning. This might seem daunting to them at first. However, this is something easily overcome by careful analysis of the local organization within the nonfiction text in question.

Instructors can point out that, unlike fiction, nonfiction does not embed the main point or meaning of the text within a narrative or through artistic word choices but clearly presents the central theme. This makes the author's intention more direct and clear and is done through a variety of methods depending on the voice and goals of the reader. When reading nonfiction, instructors should have the students look for clues indicating what the author is saying and objectives behind what's being said. Is the author seeking to argue a point, disprove a point, or simply educate the reader? Asking these questions will help the students look at how the text is organized to find these answers.

Instructors must clarify that nonfiction writing revolves around a central idea and supporting information. Students can point out the central idea by looking at the opening of the text to see if there are any direct statements or a question presented. Throughout the reading, instructors can ask students if there are recurring statements or ideas. Does the author return to an initial statement/idea? Or is the author simply writing information? If the author keeps returning to a key statement, it may indicate that their focus is on this idea. From here, the structure of supporting information will reveal even more.

Supporting information fills the majority of the nonfiction text. If the author is just reflecting on something, students should note how the author populates the text with details or how and why they think a certain way. Alternatively, if the author is trying to prove a point, the information will present and explain evidence to corroborate their claim. Some of the patterns for organizing information include sequence, cause and effect, compare and contrast, description, and problem and solution. Having students identify and group the supporting information into one of these categories will help them grasp the author's motive and gain insight from the overall piece.

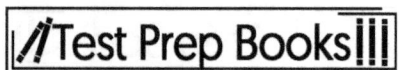

Using Evidence from Nonfiction Texts

Literal and Figurative Meanings

It is important when evaluating informational texts to consider the use of both literal and figurative meanings. The words and phrases an author chooses to include in a text must be evaluated. How does the word choice affect the meaning and tone? By recognizing the use of literal and figurative language, a reader can more readily ascertain the message or purpose of a text. **Literal** word choice is the easiest to analyze as it represents the usual and intended way a word or phrase is used. It is also more common in informational texts because it is used to state facts and definitions. While **figurative language** is typically associated with fiction and poetry, it can be found in informational texts as well. The reader must determine not only what is meant by the figurative language in context, but also how the author intended it to shape the overall text.

Inferences in Informational Texts

Inference refers to the reader's ability to understand the unwritten text, i.e., "read between the lines" in terms of an author's intent or message. The strategy asks that a reader not take everything he or she reads at face value but instead, add their own interpretation of what the author seems to be trying to convey. A reader's ability to make inferences relies on their ability to think clearly and logically about the text. It does not ask that the reader make wild speculations or guess about the material but demands that he or she be able to come to a sound conclusion about the material.

An author's use of less literal words and phrases requires readers to make more inference when they read. Since inference involves **deduction**—deriving conclusions from ideas assumed to be true—there's more room for interpretation. Still, critical readers who employ inference, if careful in their thinking, can arrive at the logical, sound conclusions the author intends.

Questioning has immeasurable value in the reading process. Answering questions about a text gives purpose for reading to students and focuses them on reading to learn information. Similarly, generating questions about a text for others to answer enables a student to analyze what is important to learn in the text and glean summarizing skills. Keeping Bloom's Taxonomy in mind, teachers can scaffold students toward increased critical thinking capabilities. Bloom's Taxonomy shows the hierarchy of learning progressing through the following stages:

- Remembering
- Understanding
- Applying
- Analyzing
- Evaluating
- Creating

Textual Evidence in Informational Text

Once a reader has determined an author's thesis or main idea, he or she will need to understand how textual evidence supports interpretation of that thesis or main idea. Test takers will be asked direct questions regarding an author's main idea and may be asked to identify evidence that would support those ideas. This will require test takers to comprehend literal and figurative meanings within the text passage, be able to draw inferences from provided information, and be able to separate important evidence from minor supporting detail. It's often helpful to skim test questions and answer options prior to critically reading informational text; however, test takers should avoid the temptation to solely look

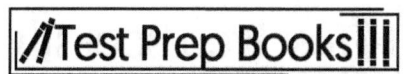

for the correct answers. Just trying to find the "right answer" may cause test takers to miss important supporting textual evidence. Making a mental note of test questions is only helpful as a guide when reading.

After identifying an author's thesis or main idea, a test taker should look at the supporting details that the author provides to back up their assertions, identifying those additional pieces of information that help expand the thesis. From there, test takers should examine the additional information and related details for credibility, the author's use of outside sources, and be able to point to direct evidence that supports the author's claims. It's also imperative that test takers be able to identify what is strong support and what is merely additional information that is nice to know but not necessary. Being able to make this differentiation will help test takers effectively answer questions regarding an author's use of supporting evidence within informational text.

Differentiating the Text Features and Formats of Various Texts

Comprehending Fiction and Literary Genres

Some important story elements in teaching reading comprehension include character, plot, problem/solution, and setting. Some inferential aspects of reading comprehension are mood, tone, theme, point of view, and voice. These elements are more difficult to teach and for students to master. Repetition and understanding improves mastery of these inferential aspects, particularly when they are broken into independent lessons.

Genre is a method of categorizing literature by form, content, style, and technique. When selections of literature share enough characteristics and literary elements, they are classified into the same genre. Genre is more than just a categorization system, though; genre identifies literature by its communicative purpose. Authors write to accomplish any of a variety of social purposes: to inform, to explain, to entertain, to persuade, to maintain relationships, and so on. All types of texts fall into one of the following five genres: fiction, nonfiction, poetry, drama, and folklore. Each of these has a variety of subgenres. A particular piece of writing may fall into more than one genre or subgenre.

A variety of texts must be used to teach literature and reading. Folklore and poetry both have aspects to enhance comprehension. Poetry teaches lyrical reading and emphasis; it is written with specific structure and rhythm. There are many types of poetry, such as ballads, lyrics, couplets, epics, and sonnets. Poetry teaches students about adhering to punctuation while reading and allows students to read with pauses. A great teaching strategy to employ with poetry lessons is the use of blank poetry books that students can use to take notes and create their own specific poems. Poetry contains similes, personification, and onomatopoeia; therefore, poems are a great way to teach imagery and figurative language.

Drama, or plays, can emphasize voice, and gives students the option to take on a role of a character. One way to teach drama is to divide students into groups and host a reader's theater. Students and teachers have a lot of fun preparing to present a play in front of the class. Prose text covers a wide range of literature from novels, to folklore, to biographies. Developing a unit dedicated to the various types of folklore (short stories, tall tales, myth, legend, and fantasy) can be creative and fun for students. Autobiographies, biographies, and historical fiction can help teach facts. Providing students with the

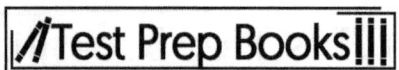

opportunity to research a person in history and present the findings to the class develops comprehension, presentation, speaking, writing, and research skills.

Recognizing Different Genres

Reading is fundamental to learning. Reading nurtures imagination, critical thinking, communication skills, and social competence. Many children are drawn to the allure of reading and often their attention is captivated by a certain type of book or books about a particular personal interest. It is important to introduce them to an eclectic selection of text types. Cultural knowledge, a more intricate worldview, and a host of new vocabulary can be built through the experience of diverse literature. Reading a wide range of writing styles brings students into contact with many characters and lifestyles. Reading varied texts sparks different emotions in a child and teaches a variety of means of expression. In this way, children deepen social and emotional skills. In short, reading a wide variety of texts produces a well-rounded education and prepares children for their experience of the world.

Fiction

Fiction is imaginative text that is invented by the author. Fiction is characterized by the following literary elements:

- **Characters**: The people, animals, aliens, or other living figures the story is about
  - **Setting**: The location, surroundings, and time the story takes place in
  - **Conflict**: A dilemma the characters face either internally or externally
  - **Plot**: The sequence and the rise and fall of excitement in the action of a story
  - **Resolution**: The solution to the conflict that is discovered as a result of the story
  - **Point of view**: The lens through which the reader experiences the story
  - **Theme**: The moral to the story or the message the author is sending to the reader

Historical Fiction

Historical fiction is a story that occurs in the past and uses a realistic setting and authentic time period characters. Historical fiction usually has some historically accurate events mixed and balanced with invented plot and characters.

Science Fiction

Science fiction is an invented story that occurs in the future or an alternate universe. It often deals with space, time travel, robots, or aliens, and highly-advanced technology.

Fantasy

Fantasy is a subgenre of fiction that involves magic or supernatural elements and/or takes place in an imaginary world. Examples include talking animals, superheroes rescuing the day, or characters taking on a mythical journey or quest.

Mystery and Adventure

Mystery fiction is a story that involves a puzzle or crime to be solved by the main characters. The mystery is driven by suspense and foreshadowing. The reader must sift through clues and distractions to solve the puzzle with the protagonist. **Adventure stories** are driven by the risky or exciting action that happens in the plot.

Text Types and Structures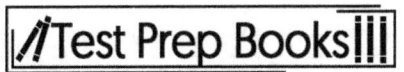

Realistic and Contemporary Fiction
Realistic fiction depends on the author portraying the world without speculation. The characters are ordinary, and the action could happen in real life. The conflict often involves growing up, family life, or learning to cope with some significant emotion or challenge.

Nonfiction Literature
Nonfiction literature is text that is true and accurate in detail. Nonfiction can cover virtually any topic in the natural world. Nonfiction writers conduct research and carefully organize facts before writing. Nonfiction has the following subgenres:

- **Informational Text**: This is text written to impart information to the reader. It may have literary elements such as charts, graphs, indexes, glossaries, or bibliographies.

- **Persuasive Text**: This is text that is meant to sway the reader to have a particular opinion or take a particular action.

- **Biographies and autobiographies**: This is text that tells intimate details of someone's life. If an author writes the text about someone else, it is a biography. If the author writes it about himself or herself, it is an autobiography.

- **Communicative text**: This is text used to communicate with another person. This includes such texts as emails, formal and informal letters, and tweets. This content often consists of two-sided dialogue between people.

Drama
Drama is any writing that is intended to be performed in front of an audience, such as plays, and TV and movie scripts. Dialogue and action are central to convey the author's theme. **Comedy** is any drama designed to be funny or lighthearted. **Tragedy** is any drama designed to be serious or sad.

Poetry
Poetry is text that is written in verse and has a rhythmic cadence. It often involves descriptive imagery, rhyming stanzas, and beautiful mastery of language. It is often personal, emotional, and introspective. Poetry is often considered a work of art.

Folklore
Folklore is literature that has been handed down from generation to generation by word of mouth. Folklore is not based in fact but in unsubstantiated beliefs. It is often very important to a culture or custom. The following are some common types of folklore:

- **Fairy Tales:** These are usually written for children and often carry a moral or universal truth. They are stories written about fairies or other magical creatures.

- **Fables:** Similar to fairy tales, fables are written for children and include tales of supernatural people or animals that speak like people. They often are built around a moral lesson.

- **Myths:** These tales are often about the gods, include symbolism, and may involve historical events and reveal human behavior. Sometimes they tell how historical things came about.

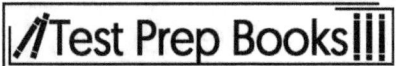

- **Legends:** Exaggerated and only partially truthful, these are tales of heroes and significant events.

- **Tall Tales:** Often funny stories and sometimes set in the Wild West, these are tales that contain extreme exaggeration and were never true.

Literary Response and Analysis Skills

Literary elements can be considered features or characteristics of fiction, but they are really more of a way that readers can examine a text for the purpose of analysis and understanding the meaning. The elements contribute to a reader's literary interpretation of a passage as to how they function to convey the central message of a work. The most common literary elements used for analysis are presented below.

Point of View
The **point of view** is the position the narrator takes when telling the story in prose. If a narrator is incorporated in a drama, the point of view may vary; in poetry, point of view refers to the position the speaker in a poem takes.

First Person
The **first-person point of view** is when the writer uses the word *I* in the text. Poetry often uses first person, e.g., William Wordsworth's "I Wandered Lonely as a Cloud." Two examples of prose written in first person are Suzanne Collins's *The Hunger Games* and Anthony Burgess's *A Clockwork Orange*.

Second Person
The **second person point of view** is when the writer uses the pronoun *you*. It is not widely used in prose fiction, but as a technique, it has been used by writers such as William Faulkner in *Absalom, Absalom!* and Albert Camus in *The Fall*. It is more common in poetry—e.g., Pablo Neruda's "If You Forget Me."

Third Person
Third person point of view is when the writer utilizes pronouns such as *him, her*, or *them*. It may be the most utilized point of view in prose as it provides flexibility to an author and is the one with which readers are most familiar. There are two main types of third person used in fiction. **Third person omniscient** uses a narrator that is all-knowing, relating the story by conveying and interpreting thoughts/feelings of all characters. In **third person limited**, the narrator relates the story through the perspective of one character's thoughts/feelings, usually the main character.

Selecting Appropriate Texts to Reflect the Backgrounds of All Learners

Choosing Multicultural and Diverse Texts

In recent years, there has been a growing emphasis on including diverse texts in the classroom. Diverse texts are books that include characters from minority groups. There are two central reasons for this change. First, students have an easier time relating to characters who share their culture and background; hence, diverse texts help students from minority groups feel included in the classroom and engage with the readings. Diverse texts empower minority students by giving them representation in the classroom, and they also help majority students expand their horizons and develop cultural awareness.

Here are some important criteria to consider when choosing diverse texts for the classroom.

- The book should depict cultural differences accurately. Books that reinforce stereotypes or contain false information will do more harm than good.

- While the diversity of the students in your classroom can guide your choice of books, it should not limit the scope of the diverse literature you choose. Books about any culture in your community, country, or even the world will help students understand and empathize with other people.

- One purpose of diverse literature is to teach children how to correctly interact with people from different cultures. Books should model positive interactions and/or provide meaningful engagement with social issues.

Evaluating Student Interest for Text Selection

While diverse literature is an essential component of any curriculum, it is best to intersperse these texts with books that feature characters and settings that are familiar to the majority of your students. Since students are most engaged when they can relate to the characters about whom they are reading, not every book needs to be about different cultures.

Teachers should also take their students' interests into account when choosing texts. Consider the surrounding community, as well as any common interests that your students share. Do most of your students live on farms, or are you teaching in an urban community? Are your students always talking about a certain topic or animal? Think about your students' interests, and then choose books that involve those issues.

Print and Nonprint Texts for Instructional Use

Evaluating Texts for Instructional Use

To find appropriate texts for their classrooms, teachers can consult lists designed to help them choose high-quality materials. To analyze sources that provide book recommendations, use the same criteria as you use to evaluate sources of reading research (discussed in the first section). Reputable sources of recommendations include reference books, resources provided by your state or school district, and government websites. For example, the Library of Congress offers lists of high-quality books for readers of all ages.

Teachers can also evaluate texts by researching the publisher. Some presses have a record of publishing excellent teaching material; for example, Macmillan/McGraw-Hill and Scholastic both publish high-quality books that are often used in classrooms. Browsing the websites of these and other respected publishers can help you locate good reading material.

Additionally, awards are a useful way of determining whether a book is high quality. For example, the **Newberry Medal** is an annual award that honors the best children's book of the year. The **Horn Book Awards** also judge books for young readers, and they offer awards in categories ranging from picture books to poetry. These are highly competitive awards, so looking at award winners and finalists is a great way to find quality literature. Awards may be particularly useful when vetting books that are only a year or two old, as these texts may not yet appear on reading lists.

Teachers should also choose books that feature age-appropriate topics. Books that include violence or other disturbing content are not good choices for young readers; however, texts that touch on these issues may be useful for older students. For example, a book about the Holocaust would be inappropriate for a first grade classroom, but it could be useful for teaching high school students about history and starting discussions about topics like politics and race.

Illustrations are also an important part of a text, particularly for young readers. The best books have high-quality illustrations that further the meaning of the text instead of detracting from it or confusing readers. Avoid resources with pictures that do not accurately represent the text, as they will mislead students. Drawings that are overly flashy and distracting can also prevent students from focusing on their reading.

Selecting Complex, Grade-Appropriate Texts

Evaluating Reading Levels and Text Complexity

Texts should not be too hard or too easy for students. But how can teachers evaluate text complexity to ensure that they are giving their students appropriate materials? There are quantitative and qualitative methods of determining a text's level.

Quantitative measures attempt to objectively calculate the difficulty of a text. The most common quantitative measures are readability formulas, or mathematical equations that strive to calculate the difficulty of a text. **Fry's formula** is a common readability formula that requires teachers to count the number of sentences and syllables in three random passages of one hundred words each. They then average each number, and chart the two numbers on a Fry graph. The **Fry graph** uses the numbers to produce a suggested grade level for the text. While this method is a useful tool for estimating a text's complexity, teachers should take it with a grain of salt; Fry's formula does not account for variation within grade levels and the text's qualitative factors.

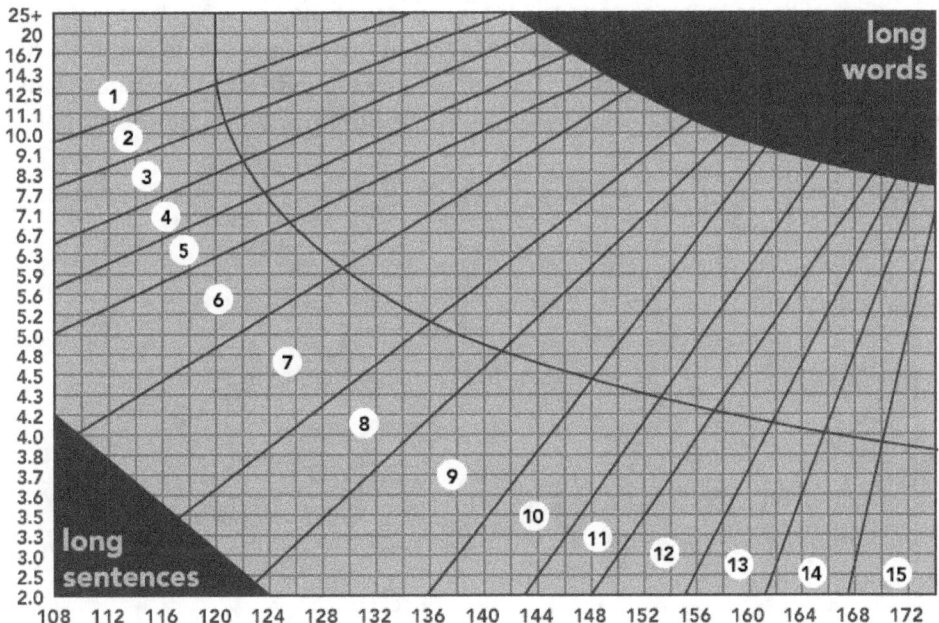

J at English Wikipedia, Public domain, via Wikimedia Commons,
https://upload.wikimedia.org/wikipedia/commons/4/47/Fry_Graph.png

The other common quantitative measures are **Lexile text measures**. Like Fry's formula, these measures rate texts based on sentence length and word complexity. However, the **Lexile method** utilizes a database of text rankings instead of having teachers do the math themselves. It also gives texts a numerical rating from 0L to 2000L (L stands for Lexile) instead of a grade level.

Qualitative measures identify subjective elements that affect the text's complexity. Below are some qualitative criteria that teachers can use to determine complexity.

- **Predictable structures** make texts easier to grasp, and they are especially useful in material intended for young children. For example, many fairy tales and children's books repeat questions and phrases. These predictable elements make the text less complicated, as children get into the pattern of the story and do not have to approach each repetition as an entirely new element.

- **Vocabulary** also determines a text's difficulty, and it cannot always be detected by quantitative measures. For example, the word "daft" consists of just one syllable, but it is clearly a more obscure word than "cat." However, Fry's formula would count the two words as the same level. Hence, teachers should skim the material to ensure the vocabulary is at an appropriate level. While texts should include some vocabulary words that will be new to students, an excess of new vocabulary renders reading so frustrating that students are likely to lose interest.

- Teachers should also consider the level of **background knowledge** required to understand a text. If easily learned background information is required (for example, basic historical context), teachers can present it to students before they begin to read a book. But if the background knowledge is complicated or far above the students' grade level, the book is not a good fit.

- Lastly, the **level of meaning** refers to how much abstract thought a text requires. Some texts only require students to understand the literal events of the book. More complex books, however, demand that students use abstract thought to make inferences and evaluate events. High levels of symbolism and abstract thought will be too difficult for younger students, while books that require only literal interpretation will be boring to more mature students.

Practice Quiz

1. What is the advantage of teaching students to use either a table of contents or index?
    a. They can transfer those skills to using the glossary.
    b. It familiarizes them with the text and allows them to independently find sections of a text.
    c. It's the first thing any reader should read in a new text.
    d. It teaches them how they can organize their own work.

2. A student encountering a typographic feature, such as bold or italics, can assume which of the following?
    a. The information is important.
    b. The concept is difficult to understand.
    c. The word is new.
    d. The word can be found in the table of contents.

3. A post-reading class discussion about a text may help students better identify which element that would otherwise be inferred?
    a. Supporting details
    b. Theme
    c. Thesis statement
    d. Conclusion

See answers on the next page.

Answer Explanations

1. B: The goal of teaching students how to use the table of contents or index is so they can use it often, familiarize themselves with sections of the text, and be able to find important parts on their own. Although teaching students to use a glossary is discussed here, it is in terms of identifying and defining vocabulary in the text, not as a transferable skill learned independently as a by-product of understanding a table of contents or index; therefore, Choice A is incorrect. Choice C is incorrect; it is among the first things a reader should review, but that's not emphasized here. Choice D is incorrect because although a table of contents or index may be an example of how organization works in larger texts, it does not teach students how to organize their own work.

2. A: The primary reason text is in bold or italics is to draw attention to its significance. A change in typographic feature does not indicate difficult information in a passage, so Choice B is incorrect. Choice C is incorrect because although the words may be vocabulary words, not all vocabulary words are new. A change in the typographic feature does not indicate a word is found in the table of contents, so Choice D is incorrect.

3. B: The theme of a text is often inferred rather than explicitly stated. Students who are adept at identifying concrete information may not yet be skilled at inferring ideas, but in a class-wide discussion, students benefit from one another's interpretations and a teacher who leads the discussion. Supporting details, Choice A, are concrete and not inferred. Choice C, the thesis statement, is also identifiable as a clear and specific statement that doesn't require inference or interpretation. Conclusion, Choice D, would be explicitly stated, not inferred in the text.

Reading Assessment and Evaluation

Screening, Diagnosis, Progress Monitoring, and Other Outcome Measures

Assessing Reading

Norm-Referenced Assessments
Norm-referenced assessments are formal tests that compare students' scores to state or national averages. They provide each student's score with a percentile, and they can be used to screen struggling students.

Two common norm-referenced assessments are the SAT and ACT. These tests measure students' abilities in reading, writing, and math. They then calculate each student's score as both a number and a percentile.

Criterion-Referenced Assessments
Criterion-referenced assessments may be formal or informal. These tests compare students' skills to predetermined levels of competency and are typically administered multiple times a year to measure student progress.

One example of a criterion-referenced assessment is the **Informal Reading Inventory**. This assessment tests students' abilities to read and understand texts at four levels. The Independent Level is the level of text that a student can read unassisted and comprehend with 90 to 100% accuracy. The Instructional Level is the level of text that is best suited for use in the classroom: the student needs a teacher's help to completely understand the passage but can comprehend about 70 to 85% of the material. A text at Frustration Level is too difficult; the student's reading comprehension is below 70 percent. Finally, the Hearing Capacity Level is the level of text that the student can comprehend with more than 70% accuracy when it is read aloud. Teachers typically use the Informal Reading Inventory at the first of the year to screen for struggling students, then they administer it several times throughout the year to track their students' progress.

Performance-Based Assessments
Performance-based assessments measure a student's ability to apply skills. These assessments require higher-level thinking, not just memorization. For example, students might write an evaluative essay to show that they understand a text.

The essay is a common performance-based assessment. Instead of simply stating the facts they learned in class, students demonstrate their ability to interact with information by creating a compelling argument.

Purposes for Assessments
Screening is a preventative attempt to identify students who are at risk of falling behind grade level. These tests are typically administered at the start of the year with the aim of offering struggling students supplemental help.

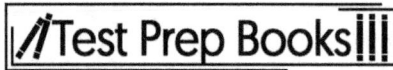

Reading Assessment and Evaluation

Diagnostic assessments measure specific skills, such as a student's ability to sound out the letter "b." These assessments may be formal exams or informal observations in class.

Progress monitoring assessments track student progress during the academic year. These tests may be used only with struggling students, or with the class as a whole. They help teachers learn whether their students have mastered the material and thereby know whether to review or move on.

Outcome assessments (or **high stakes assessments**) take place once a year and are used to assess the teacher and curriculum as well as the students. Staff and parents can compare students' scores and class averages to state or national averages. By doing so, they can determine whether the curriculum and/or teacher are leading to student success.

Oral and Written Assessment Practices

Emergent Readers' Skills

Entry-level assessments, progress monitoring, and summative assessments need to be administered in order to determine students' print awareness, letter recognition, and alphabetic principle knowledge to identify misconceptions that can be remediated in future lessons. Formal and informal assessment methods are as follows:

- **Print awareness** is easily assessed through observation. Teachers can give students a book and ask them to demonstrate their tracking and orientation knowledge. Similarly, teachers can ask students to identify parts of a book, such as its title or page numbers.

- The **Concepts About Print (CAP) test** assesses a student's print awareness. The CAP test is administered one-on-one, typically at the beginning and middle of a student's kindergarten year. During the CAP test, the teacher asks a student questions about a book's print. The teacher records the student's responses to the questions asked on a standardized rubric. This helps to identify specific areas of weakness for each student in terms of print awareness. These areas can then be reinforced and retaught in future lessons.

Planned Observations
The **Observation Survey** created by Marie Clay, can be beneficial in the assessment of a student's letter recognition and alphabetic principle knowledge. The Observation Survey includes six literacy tasks:

1. Letter Identification
2. Concepts About Print
3. Writing Vocabulary
4. Hearing and Recording Sounds in Words
5. Text Reading
6. Word Test

During such assessments, a student may be asked to identify a letter's name, its sound, rhyming pairs, isolated initial/final phonemes, blending of compound words/syllables, and word segments, or to add or delete phonemes in words. Similarly, teachers can say a letter and ask students to write that letter on a sheet of paper. The teacher records student responses. In this way, the teacher can identify the skills that have not yet been mastered by a single student, small group, or entire class. The teacher can then use any of the aforementioned strategies to reinforce those skills within individuals, small groups, or whole-class instruction.

Ongoing Assessment of Reading Skills and Strategies

Letter-Sound Assessments

During phoneme and **letter-sound correspondence assessments**, teachers point to random letters or phonemes. The student is to then say the sound of the letter or phoneme and the teacher records the student's responses. Letter-sound combinations and phonemes with which a student, group, or class needs additional instruction and/or practice can be identified. The teacher can use this information to create lessons that emphasize the identified letter-sound correspondences and/or phonemes.

Phonics Assessments

Examples to test a student's ability to decode words or readily read sight words include Sylvia Green's Informal Word Analysis Inventory, Test of Word Reading Efficacy (TOWRE), and the CORE Phonics Survey. In these types of assessments, students are given a list of words and/or phonics patterns. Initially, high-frequency words that follow predictable phonics patterns are presented. Examples of **predictable phonics patterns** may include blending, word patterns, digraphs, etc. The words presented become more challenging as a student masters less difficult words. For example, a child may be assessed on their ability to decode nonsense words. The nonsense word assessments progress from decoding common sounds to less common sounds. Multisyllabic words within the assessments can reveal how well learners can chunk word parts through syllabication. As with other assessments discussed, the student's responses are recorded on a teacher's record sheet. In this way, the teacher can identify which word analysis principles and sight words a single student, a group of students, or an entire class is having difficulty with. These sight words, word parts, letter combinations, blending patterns, and/or syllabication principles can then be reinforced, retaught, reviewed, and practiced in future lessons. Additionally, the results of the assessment can be used to form instructional groups.

Informal Word Analysis Inventories

These can be used to assess encoding (spelling) of single-syllable words in the traditional manner. Students write the words that are read aloud by their teacher on a sheet of paper. In the early stages of spelling development, students are assessed on lists of words that are common to everyday language, share a word pattern or theme, and/or follow common orthographic patterns. The word lists become more complex as students demonstrate proficiency. The teacher can then plan instruction that targets the letter combinations and patterns with which students are struggling. Such assessments can also be used to form instructional groups of students who share the same approximate developmental stage of spelling to better facilitate differentiated instruction.

As a general rule of thumb, isolated phonics tests should be given every four to six weeks. Spelling assessments can be given weekly or biweekly. Remediation should be implemented when students miss two or more questions on a five-question assessment and three or more questions on a ten-question assessment.

Contextualized Decoding Assessments

Despite the popularity of isolated decoding assessments, decoding should also be assessed in context. The **Word Recognition in Context** subtest of the Phonological Awareness Literacy Screening (PALS) is an example of an assessment that can be used for this purpose. During such assessments, passages that

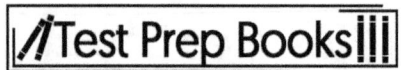

can be read by a student with 90 to 97% accuracy at acceptable rates are selected. The student reads these passages aloud to the teacher.

By analyzing students' approaches to figuring out unknown words and students' errors when reading a grade-appropriate passage, teachers are better able to determine which of the following three decoding strategies to emphasize during instruction:

- **Meaning cues** should be emphasized when a student fails to use context, story background, or pictures to assist in the decoding of new words.

- **Structural cues** are emphasized when a student does not use grammar or syntax to figure out an unknown word.

- **Visual cues** are emphasized when a student does not use grapheme or phoneme information to decode an unknown word. For example, a student may only read the beginning, middle, or end of words correctly (e.g., read hat as cat). A student may leave off a suffix or use incorrect yet similar letter combinations, indicating that visual cues need to be retaught.

Spelling Assessments

Similarly, spelling should be assessed within the context of a student's writing samples. When a student's spelling is assessed in the context of a writing assignment, a teacher is able to detect patterns of misconceptions and areas that need remediation. Not only can such assessments be used to detect the proper encoding of words, but also a student's vocabulary, diction, and syntax. By using a rubric, teachers are better able to determine which developmental stage of spelling (the pre-phonetic stage, the semiphonetic stage, the phonetic stage, the transitional stage, and the conventional stage) of each student. Spelling instruction that targets each student's individual strengths, weaknesses, and developmental stage of spelling can then be created and implemented by the teacher.

Please note that once a student's areas of need are determined, any of the previously suggested phonics, sight word, or spelling strategies can be used for remediation and re-teaching of the identified skills.

Interpreting Student Data to Inform Small-Group Instruction

Assessments can be used to gather diagnostic data regarding students' reading progress. These assessments can highlight which material needs to be taught and tested again in order for the student to overcome various reading difficulties. Based on the results of these assessments, students can then be placed into small groups for instruction that is tailored to their needs.

Diagnostic reading data can be collected in a few ways. Formal and informal assessments will help teachers to determine deficits in learning progression that should be addressed. For example, a formal assessment may include selected-response questions that can be graded quickly for accuracy. Informal assessments may also include selected-response questions that can better enable the teacher to hone in on the specific concepts that need to be reinforced.

Small groups should be created by putting together students who have similar struggles. If a formal assessment shows that five students in the class are struggling to understand pronouns, it would be beneficial to place those students together in a small group where practicing pronouns is the focus. If during an informal assessment multiple students get the same questions about phonetics incorrect, grouping them together to work on vocabulary assignments would be appropriate. This is a form of differentiated instruction. Differentiated instruction allows students to tackle reading principles in the way that works best for them. It acknowledges that classrooms are full of students with diverse needs. The group is taught as a whole, but it is often necessary for students to use different learning strategies based on their needs.

When grouping students together for individualized learning, the groups should be formed based on the skills being addressed rather than on scores. The score may be taken into account when considering pacing and question complexity, but it should not be the main focus. For example, multiple students may have scored 70% on a benchmark exam; however, that does not mean that they missed the same 30% of the exam questions. Their missed questions could be on a variety of concepts. As the students' needs change, so should the groupings. Reassessing continuously, whether daily or weekly, allows students to continue developing the skills that may require extra studying.

Interpreting Student Data to Inform Whole-Group Instruction

Similar to small-group instruction, whole-group instruction can be informed through formal and informal assessments. These assessments are used to determine a student's progress toward a set learning objective. Through these assessments, instructors can identify patterns and trends in performance. This is done by keeping track of what students are successfully and unsuccessfully answering. If only a few students are struggling with a subject, small-group instruction would be appropriate. However, if a large number of students are failing to grasp a concept, it would be beneficial to continue to focus on that concept during whole-group instruction.

Assessing where the class is should be happening frequently. The grouping of students, whether it be in whole groups or small groups, is determined entirely by the ongoing assessments. The lessons should be modeled and adjusted according to what the assessments reveal about student understanding. After reteaching is implemented, additional assessments can be used to monitor progress. The teacher should continue to reinforce strengths and support weaknesses based on these results.

Assessments should also inform the teacher about the style of instruction that works best for the whole group. The type of assessment may also align with the concepts being learned. If the students need reinforcement on reading comprehension, activities that help them visualize what they are reading may help. Additionally, asking students to paraphrase and summarize texts may be a good test to show their level of understanding.

Prompting students to ask questions and openly discuss concepts may be helpful for whole-group instruction. Strong discussion allows for collaboration and communication, which are vital skills for learning. Reading aloud may also aid in developing reading strategies. Various forms of multimedia, such as videos or slideshows, may also be an interactive way to change up whole-group instruction. Consider peer teaching as well, since it can provide the whole group with an alternative perspective other than that of the teacher. This encourages student engagement, which helps improve reading skills. Students who feel interested and engaged in learning are more likely to succeed at reaching their learning objectives.

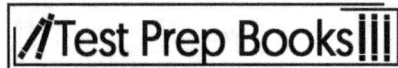

Using Data from Reading and Writing Assessments to Differentiate Instruction

Educational Measurement and Evaluation

Being able to effectively evaluate student performance enables teachers to develop the best instructions to help their students reach their potential. Reading assessments are key to identifying individual strengths and weaknesses, so both formal and informal assessments should be used in the classroom. Being able to successfully gauge individual reading levels means looking at essential performance indicators of rate and accuracy.

An **oral fluency assessment** should be used to see how students approach reading as a whole. This assessment examines the number of words the student can read within one minute. A text relative to the student's level should be used. For beginning learners, the difficulty of the text can be below their initial level too. Based on how many correct words the student reads, an instructor can determine how advanced they are in developing reading skills. The number of times students incorrectly read words and the length of time it takes for them to read the text will also determine their level of fluency. Fluency assessments also consider the way in which a student reads, whether the language flows or is stalled.

There are four levels of fluency. Levels 1 and 2 reflect nonfluency; these students will need more instruction to hone their reading skills, which may entail various kinds of differentiated instruction. Level 1 is the lowest; these students read word by word and lack tone in their reading. Levels 3 and 4 represent fluent readership. Level 4 reflects the students' ability to read phrases consistently and accurately without having to repeat words. Multiple errors in the reading as well as repetitions may also occur.

When considering the results of such assessments, it's important for instructors to be observant and note where in the reading students struggled and, in addition, to analyze why the reading issues exist. Did certain words confuse the student, or did the student just seem uncertain of their own abilities? Did certain grammatical phrasing confuse the reader? Asking questions like these will help find root problems and enable the specialist to construct actionable plans to steer improvement. It's important to remember that such issues can indicate learning disabilities, so identifying all these issues early is very important. These assessments should also be used to track student progress and assess how effective instruction is in overcoming core issues.

Diagnosing Reading Needs

Assessments are useful for identifying which students may be struggling with certain criteria as well as the specific areas of difficulty. Assessments can also indicate how well the material is being presented or provide vital clues on how to modify an individual student's instruction to help them grasp the content better. Generally, two types of assessments are used: informal and formal.

Informal assessments are not planned and lack a typical format or timeline. They can be as simple as watching and listening to how the students respond to answers in class or perform classwork. Observation is key. The instructor should be perceptive to how students not only respond to reading and language concepts but also to how they are interpreting them. If a student isn't understanding something such as a cultural reading concept, it may indicate that a more in-depth explanation is required. This will help the teacher adapt the instruction to enable the student to self-correct their own performance.

Formal assessments are partially based on observation, but are planned and implemented with the design to see how students respond to specific stimuli. They give a clearer indication of where students' weaknesses lie or whether they are on point in grasping the material. There are two primary methods for conducting formal assessments. The most conventional is a simple pencil-and-paper test in which students read prewritten questions and respond to them in writing. These physical answers provide a direct window into what the students know and how their reading comprehension is progressing.

Performance assessments are a little less concrete but can provide a lot of insight into the student's mindset and reactions that are more three-dimensional than a written assessment. This method does not use written responses, but instead analyzes students' performance in response to reading questions or activities. When giving performance assessments, it's important to bear in mind key questions: Does the student understand what they just read, did they seem uncomfortable when presenting their answer, and how accurate was their response? From here, new teaching strategies can be implemented, or the instructor can identify ways to provide specialized assistance to boost students' skills.

Accelerating the Development of Reading Skills

Whether an instructor uses informal or formal assessment, data will be produced from the assessment. This data, both written or gained through observation, is highly valuable in diagnosing whether to change teaching methods in order to accelerate students' reading skills development. Data-driven instruction guides reading improvement for all students simply because the data provides clear indications of where students are facing reading challenges or demonstrating strengths.

Differentiated instruction acknowledges that, while a group of students may be learning the same subject, the way each student learns and processes the subject is different. This technique looks at the different learning methods and reading areas that students respond best to in order to effect change. Therefore, an educator can then tailor, or differentiate, lessons to build on these skills and expedite the learning process. Differentiated instruction is divided into interest-based and ability-based instruction.

Much of a student's performance is based on their interest in the subject at hand. Sometimes a student may show difficulty reading because he or she isn't engaged in the material. One way to encourage reading growth is to allow students to choose their learning activities. This will give students ownership over their own education, enabling them to have fun while learning and to use specific activities they feel help them improve their reading abilities. For example, students more interested in visual activities may find reading more beneficial than listening to oral reading exercises.

Ability-based differentiation focuses on three core focus areas that determine reading proficiency and build skill. The first area of focus examines students' conceptual understanding of reading. If a teacher uses vocabulary or reading comprehension exercises in class, they will be able to examine how students are performing and modify instruction to address any confusion. This can also indicate students' preferences as well. The second differentiation looks at how students analyze and use the reading. Instructors must look at how students respond to questions and whether their interpretation is accurate. The final differentiation looks at how students evaluate and perform reading, creating a reaction that responds to the reading. The third differentiation looks at interpretation with the added step of using this knowledge to write or say something without being prompted. Identifying issues in one of these areas will narrow down where more emphasis must be placed to improve reading skills. Each reading area will affect the other two; improving one differentiated area will impact the others.

Response to Intervention (RTI) Process

Response to Intervention Process (RTI) is a process designed to help struggling students catch up through intervention and monitoring in a general education classroom. Students who suffer from undiagnosed reading disorders, attention issues, or even ELL students struggling to learn the language may begin to fall behind the rest of the students in reading skills. RTI is an informal intervention process done by the school that focuses on utilizing research and technology to help the student "catch up" to the rest of the class. The school's RTI teams will review assessments taken of each child in the classroom to determine which students need these instructional interventions. Teachers track students through **progress monitoring**, a process that measures whether or not the interventions are making a difference.

Although there are various ways to do RTI, it is usually set up as a three-tier system of support, also known as **multi-tier system of supports (MTSS)**. The tiers below are in order of least intense to most intense.

Tier 1: High-Quality Classroom Instruction, Screening, and Group Interventions
In **Tier 1 interventions**, the entire classroom is assessed using universal screening, where everyone's skillset is measured in a general education classroom by using methods that have been proven to be effective. Students who receive Tier 1 support are generally divided into small groups based on their skill level. Many students receive Tier 1 support because their math or reading skills are not quite at grade level. Progress of Tier 1 instruction is monitored, and many students are able to effectively catch up to grade level.

Tier 2: Targeted Interventions
Tier 2 interventions are for students who do not yet reach the potential of Tier 1 intervention. Targeted interventions give more detailed attention to the student who is struggling in addition to the regular classroom instruction. Since targeted interventions are done in addition to the regular classroom instruction, they are sometimes conducted during extracurricular activities or electives.

Tier 3: Intensive Interventions and Comprehensive Evaluation
The **Tier 3 Interventions** of the RTI process is intensive intervention. Intensive interventions are often done one-on-one or in small groups with other special-needs children. Usually only one or two students in a classroom will need this kind of instruction, so one-on-one help is more readily available for this tier.

Diagnosing Reading Difficulties

There are many factors that influence a child's language acquisition. A child's physical age, level of maturity, home and school experiences, general attitudes toward learning, and home languages are just some of the many influences on a child's literacy development. However, a child's **language acquisition** progresses through the following generalized stages:

Stage	Examples	Typical Age
Preproduction	Does not verbalize/ nods yes and no	Zero to six months
Early production	One to two word responses	Six to twelve months
Speech emergence	Produces simple sentences	One to three years
Intermediate fluency	Simple to more complex sentences	Three to five years
Advanced fluency	Near-native level of speech	Five to seven years

While this applies to language acquisition in one's home language, the very same stages apply to English language learners (ELLs). Since effective communication in any given language requires much more than a mere collection of vocabulary words that one can accurately translate, paying particular attention to each stage in language acquisition is imperative. In addition to vocabulary knowledge, language acquisition involves the study and gradual mastery of intonation, a language's dialects—if applicable—and the various nuances in a language regarding word use, expression, and cultural contexts. With time, effort, patience, and effective instructional approaches, both students and educators will begin to see progress in language acquisition.

Second language acquisition does not happen overnight. When educators take the time to study each stage and implement a variety of effective instructional approaches, progress and transition from one stage to the next will be less cumbersome and more consistent. In the early stages of language acquisition, children are often silently observing their new language environment. At these early stages, listening comprehension should be emphasized with the use of read alouds, music, and visual aids. Educators should be mindful of their vocabulary usage by consciously choosing to speak slowly and to use shorter, less complex vocabulary. Modeling during these beginning stages is also very effective. If the educator has instructed the class to open a book, the educator can open a book as a visual guide. If it is time to line up, the educator can verbally state the instruction and then walk to the door to begin the line.

During the **pre-production stage**, educators and classmates may assist ELLs by restating words or sentences that were uttered incorrectly, instead of pointing out errors. When modeling the correct language usage instead of pointing out errors, ELL learners may be less intimidated to practice their new language.

As students progress into the **early production stage**, they will benefit from exercises that challenge them to produce simple words and sentences with the assistance of visual cues. The educator should ask students to point to various pictures or symbols and produce words or sentences to describe the images they see. At the early production and **speech emergent stages**, ELL students are now ready to answer more diverse questions as they begin to develop a more complex vocabulary. Working in heterogeneous pairs and small groups with native speakers will help ELL students develop a more advanced vocabulary.

At the beginning and **intermediate fluency stages**, ELLs may be asked questions that require more advanced cognitive skills. Asking for opinions on a certain subject or requiring students to brainstorm and find ways to explain a given phenomenon are other ways to strengthen language proficiency and increase vocabulary.

When a child reaches the **advanced fluency stage**, they will be confident in social and academic language environments. This is an opportune time to introduce and/or increase their awareness of idiomatic expressions and language nuances.

World-Class Instructional Design and Assessment (WIDA) is a consortium of various departments of education throughout the United States that design and implement proficiency standards and assessments for English language learners and Spanish language learners. Primarily focusing on listening, speaking, reading, and writing, WIDA has designed and implemented English language development standards and offers professional development for educators, as well as educational research on instructional best practices. The five English language proficiency standards according to WIDA are as follows:

- Within a school environment, ELL students require communication skills for both social and instructional purposes.
- Effective communication involving information, ideas, and concepts are necessary for ELL students to be academically successful in the area of Language Arts.
- Effective communication involving information, ideas, and concepts are necessary for ELL students to be academically successful in the area of Mathematics.
- Effective communication involving information, ideas, and concepts are necessary for ELL students to be academically successful in the area of Science.
- Effective communication involving information, ideas, and concepts are necessary for ELL students to be academically successful in the area of Social Studies.

According to WIDA, mastering the understanding, interpretation, and application of the four **language domains**—listening, speaking, reading, and writing—is essential for language proficiency. Listening requires ELL students to be able to process, understand, interpret, and evaluate spoken language. Speaking proficiently allows ELL students to communicate their thoughts, opinions, and desires orally in a variety of situations and for a variety of audiences. The ability to read fluently involves the processing, understanding, interpreting, and evaluating of written language with a high level of accuracy, and writing proficiency allows ELL students to engage actively in written communication across a multitude of disciplines and for a variety of purposes.

Since language acquisition involves the ELL students, their families, their classmates, educators, principals and administrators, as well as test and curriculum developers, WIDA strives to ensure that the English Language Proficiency Standards reflect both the social and academic areas of language development.

Types of Disabilities for Literacy Development

When students display intense or specific learning difficulties with reading material, it may be indicative that they have learning disabilities. It's important for educators to understand that learning disabilities are relatively common and can be overcome. To help students do this, however, an instructor must be mindful of the types and effects of various learning disorders. Addressing these learning disabilities is crucial for early development.

Reading disorders, as they sound, are when students exhibit difficulties reading or understanding the written word. One of the most common reading disorders is **dyslexia**. A common sign of dyslexia is that the student will reverse the order of letters and thus confuse sounds or misread words. This disorder isn't a lapse in intelligence at all; many individuals can speak just fine and understand the words and principles. However, visually, they have trouble interpreting the writing. Specialized instruction focuses on giving students methods for reading text more carefully to identify what's written.

Another type of learning disorder category deals with difficulties students face when physically writing content. Students with this type of disorder may read passages without any problems, but when it comes to spelling out words and constructing sentences, there are recurring issues. This difficulty with written expression is called **dysgraphia**, which is characterized by poor handwriting and constant grammatical and spelling errors. While this may seem common in early learners, students with dysgraphia can display these issues at older age ranges. Another core aspect of dysgraphia is that students have difficulties expressing themselves in writing. While they have good ideas, they may have trouble presenting them in a logical sequence. Naturally, the instructor will want to customize the instruction for these students, focusing on writing and composition exercises to address the problem areas and help students regain confidence in their abilities.

It's important to note that disorders cannot be cured the way a doctor might treat an infection. Differentiated instruction can help address some of the core issues of learning disabilities while also boosting student morale. This process will be expedited by keeping students engaged and encouraging them throughout the process; these factors will determine how hard students strive to learn and overcome issues.

Practice Quiz

1. Which of the following is NOT true in Tier 1 interventions?
   a. The entire classroom is assessed using universal screening.
   b. Students who receive Tier 1 support are generally given one-on-one support in addition to classroom teaching.
   c. Progress of Tier 1 instruction is monitored, and many students are able to effectively catch up to grade level.
   d. Many students receive Tier 1 support because their math or reading skills are not quite at grade level.

2. Ability-based differentiation involves all EXCEPT which of the following core focus areas?
   a. Students' conceptual understanding of reading
   b. How students analyze and use a reading
   c. How students self-select appropriately-leveled readings
   d. How students evaluate and respond to reading

3. A student takes a standardized formal reading assessment and achieves a score that lands them in the 77th percentile. What does this mean?
   a. The student answered 77% of the questions correctly.
   b. The student answered 77 questions correctly.
   c. The student performed better than 77% of test takers.
   d. 77% of test takers scored higher than the student.

4. If diagnostic assessments indicate students have phonetic problems, which of the following activities would be best for the instructor to introduce?
   a. Activities that analyze the different aspects of words.
   b. Activities that help students visualize what they read.
   c. Activities that have students paraphrase and summarize texts.
   d. Activities that involve using graphic organizers to identify key points and supporting details in texts.

5. Which of the following is an example of interest-based differentiation?
   a. Grouping students who are all struggling with comprehending grade-level vocabulary words.
   b. Grouping students who are all working on reading fluency.
   c. Grouping students who are all working on sounding out unfamiliar words when reading aloud.
   d. Grouping students who are all auditory learners.

See answers on the next page.

Answer Explanations

1. B: Rather than receiving primarily one-on-one support, students who receive Tier 1 support are generally divided into small groups based on their skill level. One-on-one support is more characteristic of Tier 3 support because this format can provide a more intensive intervention.

2. C: There are three core areas of focus that ability-based differentiation addresses that determine reading proficiency and build reading skills. These include examining students' conceptual understanding of reading, how students analyze and use the reading, and how students evaluate and respond to reading. Self-selecting readings that are appropriate for the reader's level is an important skill that students develop, but it is not a hallmark of ability-based differentiation.

3. C: Percentile scores provide a means of score comparisons and range from 1 to 99. A student's percentile score indicates the percentage of total test takers for whom that student outperformed. For example, a student who scored in the 77th percentile achieved a score that is higher than 77% of the rest of the test cohort. A student's percentile score is different than the percentage of correct responses obtained on the test. A percentile score simply compares one student's score with the scores of all of the other students who took the test.

4. A: When students have phonetic problems, instructors should introduce activities that analyze the different aspects of words, and how to sound out words, to build familiarity with English vocabulary and structure. The other choices would be more appropriate activities to aid reading comprehension.

5. D: Interest-based differentiation is based on the concept that students' performance can be associated with their interest level in the subject or activity. Choices A, B, and C are based on performance or skill level, while Choice D is an example of interest-based differentiation. Instructors can encourage reading growth by allowing students to choose their learning activities. Students more interested in auditory activities may find listening to oral reading exercises more engaging than reading alone in their own head.

Learning Environments

Grouping Practices

Flexible Grouping and Addressing Changing Reading Needs

Another way to differentiate instruction is the use of groups and collaboration in going over or learning the reading material. In class, there are two forms of grouping instruction: teacher-based and student-based. A well-balanced and flexible learning environment will incorporate both types of grouping exercises to help students approach reading from multiple angles and practice problem-solving and critical-thinking skills. Students also strengthen social skills through flexible grouping.

Teacher-based grouping is organized by the instructor. This is the best method for introducing students to new material and exploring key concepts. Instructors may also choose to break the class up into small groups to provide instruction and work with students individually while the class is working. The goal here is to monitor students directly and provide differentiated instruction when necessary. This is the more variable of the two groupings and provides a more direct line for teacher intervention. However, students can also grasp concepts by interacting with their peers.

Student-based grouping focuses on students dictating the way the group is formed, essentially freeing the teacher to observe how they are interacting with others and approaching reading topics. Students can be given the option to form their groups independently or simply opening the class to a group discussion. This is different from actually lecturing because it allows students to talk about the reading subject among themselves as opposed to just listening and learning from the instructor. Posing questions for the class is a great way for students to learn correct answers and ask questions through simple conversation. Student-based groups are also excellent for school projects, allowing group members to pool their knowledge for success.

Flexible grouping relies on utilizing both teacher-based and student-based groupings throughout the instructional period. Using one more than the other isn't necessarily unbalanced, but the instructor should try to incorporate both groupings in order to broaden the students' experience. The teacher's choice in using either method should also relate to how they are implementing differentiated teaching methods. Educators can combine the use of grouping to suit activities and lessons for all areas in which students may be facing difficulties in order to boost confidence and clarify material.

Speaking and Listening, Reading, Writing, and Viewing

Integrating Language Skills in the Classroom

While there are countless creative ways to integrate language skills in the classroom, here are some of the more common methods:

Role play is an entertaining and low-stress way for students to practice speaking. Students playing store can practice vocabulary. Students acting out a book that the class has just read can practice to summarizing a text. Role play can take place with the class as a whole or in small groups.

Literature circles are groups of students who read the same text independently and meet to discuss it. The teacher groups students based on their level or interests and allows them to choose an appropriate book. The teacher may also assign each student a different role, such as leading discussion or collecting new vocabulary words. The helps keep the group on track and teaches leadership skills. Literature circles foster social connection and critical thinking skills, but they are not suitable for very young students.

Discussion circles are similar to literature circles, but they focus on discussing topics, issues, or ideas rather than the text itself. In an ESL classroom or lower grade, teachers may guide students to discuss a general topic rather than a text. For example, if the theme of the book is overcoming obstacles, students might reflect on obstacles they've encountered in their own lives and discuss their experiences. For students with more advanced language skills, discussion circles are a place to practice persuasive skills and debate more abstract topics such as issues of morality and ethical principles.

In **jigsaw discussions**, the teacher assigns each student or small group a different reading. After everyone has read their assignment, the students meet and present their findings to the group. For example, students might each read about a different country in South America before reconvening to give mini-presentations and combine their information into a travel guide. By summarizing material in front of a group, students practice comprehension, speaking, and critical thinking skills. Jigsaw discussions also help students learn to collaborate effectively, and can encourage notetaking.

Language games help students practice their language skills while providing a break from more serious class activities. Games can involve anything from Simon Says to reading a word and then drawing it for the other students to guess.

Promoting Reading Comprehension Through Writing Activities

One way to create an effective reader is to practice comprehension through writing activities. While reading should be an active process, writing forces the student to focus more clearly on spelling, sentence combination, punctuation, and other syntax practices that improve one's ability to read a difficult text. A knowledgeable writer is a knowledgeable reader, and students can practice reading through writing the text themselves. Some writing activities that propagate reading comprehension are listed below:

- Students can Write About the Texts They Read: One activity in promoting reading comprehension is to have students write about a text after they've read it. This type of writing is called a **response**, where a student will draw conclusions about a text, write about their reactions to the text, or answer questions the instructor has provided relating to the text.

- Teach Writing Skills in Relation to Reading: Comprehension can also be improved by teaching students the processes that go into writing a text, such as organizational structure or sentence construction. Teaching spelling and writing vocabulary words also increase reading fluency.

- Increase the Quantity of Student Writing: Have students write frequently. Whether it be a response to a text, lesson, or presentation, students should be consistently practicing their writing skills in order to become more familiar with language overall.

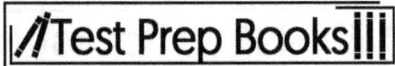

Learning Environments

Writing Mechanics

Educators must first be masters of the English language in order to teach it. Teachers serve several key roles in the classroom that all require that they know the conventions of grammar, punctuation, and spelling. Teachers are communicators. They must know how to structure their own language for clarity. They must also be able to interpret what the students are saying to accurately either affirm or revise it for correctness. Teachers are educators of language. They are the agents of change from poor-quality conventions to mastery of the concepts. Teachers are responsible for differentiating instruction so that students at all levels and aptitudes can succeed with language learning. Teachers need to be able to isolate gaps in skill sets and decide which skills need intervention in the classroom.

Teachers are evaluators. They are responsible for making key decisions about a student's educational trajectory based on their assessment of the student's capabilities.

Teachers also have great impact on how students view themselves as learners. Teachers are models. They must be superb examples of educated individuals. Just like with any other subject, people need a strong grasp of the basics of language. They will not be able to learn these things unless the teachers themselves have mastered it.

Teachers foster socialization; socialization to cultural norms and to the everyday practices of the community in which they live is of utmost importance to students' lives. These processes begin at home but continue early in a child's life at school. Teachers play a key role in guiding and scaffolding students' socialization skills. If teachers are to excel in this role, they need to be adept with the use of the English language.

Teachers need to have mastery of the conventions of English including:

- Nouns
    - Collective Nouns
    - Compound Subjects
    - Pronouns
    - Subjects, Objects, and Compounds
    - Pronoun/Noun Agreement
    - Indefinite Pronouns
    - Choosing Pronouns
    - Adjectives
    - Compound Adjectives
    - Verbs
    - Infinitives
    - Verb Tenses
    - Participles
    - Subject/Verb Agreement
    - Active/Passive Voice
    - Adverbs
    - Double Negatives
    - Comparisons
    - Double Comparisons

Learning Environments

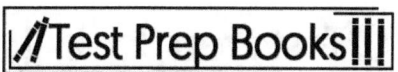

- Prepositions
- Prepositional Phrases
- Conjunctions
- Interjections
- Articles
- Types of sentences
- Subjects and Predicates
- Clauses and Phrases
- Pronoun Reference Problems
- Misplaced Modifiers
- Dangling Participial Phrases
- Punctuation
- Periods
- Commas
- Semicolons and Colons
- Parentheses and Dashes
- Quotation Marks
- Apostrophes
- Hyphens
- Question Marks
- Exclamation Points
- Capitalization
- Spelling
- Noun Plurals
- Prefixes and Suffixes
- Spelling Hurdles
- Abbreviations
- Pronunciation
- Homonyms and other easy mix-ups

Writing Development

Like with any complicated processes, writing development begins with the simplest form of indiscernible scribbles and progresses to fully formed words and, finally, to clearly written sentences and paragraphs. This is actually a complicated cognitive process that takes time and instruction to improve.

With very young students, emphasis can focus on simply making letters clear. After all, letter and word formation are the starting blocks of written language. The next phase in development can focus on actually creating words and making sure they are spelled correctly. When students are at the sentence development stage, grammar and linguistic rules become a priority. The foundations of the English language need to be firm in order for students to have good writing. When students have progressed to more advanced levels and are composing fully formed sentences with a specific purpose, it's time to incorporate content-related feedback.

Feedback at all levels of writing development is crucial; this is how students will learn to correct mistakes and strengthen growing skills. Instructor feedback must be clear while also being sensitive to the students' struggles or backgrounds. Differentiated instruction may be required to bolster students' writing skills. A good starting point for overall writing instruction is to introduce students to the stages of writing an original piece.

The goal with the stages of writing is to build on the previous work. The prewriting stage is the time for students to write down ideas and plan on how they will approach the topic at hand. The actual writing stage then dovetails on this fluidly because the student already has a framework of what the writing will focus on and how they will present information. In addition to practicing physical writing, these stages focus on critical thinking and planning skills and may lessen the student's stress before they write and receive feedback. Feedback on the initial writing, or first draft, is key. The instructor should be able to assess any difficulties and then steer the student toward improving their writing in the revision stage. After revisions, instructors should examine how effective their feedback was in helping the writing improve overall.

Effective Composing

Good writing is composed of several key elements: development, focus, clarity and coherence, grammatical proficiency, and originality. Different institutions and individual instructors will list such qualities differently, but good composition will have these basic qualities.

Strong compositions have well-developed ideas that are explained clearly throughout the piece. Good writing seems to have been planned and executed without any gaps or confusion. Through their writing, students must essentially develop an idea and line of reasoning that leave readers clear about the focus of the piece. This also means that paragraphs must be arranged in a way that they enhance and expand on the central focus of the paper, using evidence sensibly.

A writer's focus is the central point. A successful composition will not only contain a clear focus but carry the focus throughout the piece. The reader should never lose the focus or be confused by it. The way in which the content is presented throughout the text, while remaining focused on the central idea, is key. This is done by the tactical use of evidence surrounding and supporting claims relating to the central idea.

Language can be elegant and creative, but it must be used in a way the reader can understand. Much of a writer's success will depend on the coherence of the written piece. Paragraphs and the ideas within them should not be random but connect together, seamlessly blending into the next section to advance the focus of the writing. Each paragraph should strengthen the claim. Unnecessary paragraphs disrupt the flow of the writing and distract the reader, ultimately weakening the piece. Naturally, the writing should also be grammatically correct and proofed for accurate spelling and sentence structure.

Originality is the defining aspect of a well-written piece. Students should not parrot the writing style or ideas of others but instead write something that is unique. Ideas, and the way they are presented, should be fresh and approach topics in a way that offers a new perspective to the reader.

Effective Written Expression

Written expression refers to the ability of the writer to fluidly communicate meaning and purpose throughout the composition. Essentially, this refers not only to how clear the central focus of the piece is but how well the ideas surrounding the central focus are presented. If the writer can't successfully express the meaning and implications of the idea, the writing will not be strong.

Effective written expression utilizes detailed, clear communication. A writer doesn't need to unload elaborate diction throughout the paragraphs. Such an embellishment can be distracting to the reader, which actually defeats the principles behind effective writing. Sentences should be direct and emphasize language that, while engaging, remains simple enough for the audience to understand. This doesn't mean abstaining from using advanced words but rather keeping sentences direct and to the point. Students should avoid rambling line after line. Avoiding exaggerating language or overdramatic phrasing is also important. Not only can this confuse the reader, it can also harm the reader's credibility.

A simple formula for effective writing is to introduce an idea, discuss it, and then make a conclusion. This applies for the written piece as a whole but must also be used within individual paragraphs. If a writer just introduces idea after idea with no substance, the reader is left with unsubstantiated claims. Without supporting evidence to understand the view, the reader is left with only opinion. With the implementation of facts and supporting details, this opinion is strengthened. Thus, the reasoning behind the central idea is clearly executed and can be considered seriously. This helps the writer achieve credibility.

Paragraph coherence is vital for effective written expression. Paragraph sequencing and information placement are essential to streamlining the entire piece. Evidence and supporting information should be used to transition from one section to another, up to the conclusion. This enables the information to be clearly expressed. The author should strive to write in a way that, as the piece progresses, the focus becomes clearer and more convincing. By the conclusion of the written piece, the author should also restate their thesis to solidify their views and reasoning.

Recursive Steps of the Writing Process

Like with any complicated processes, writing development begins with the simplest form of indiscernible scribbles and progresses to fully formed words and, finally, to clearly written sentences and paragraphs. This is actually a complicated cognitive process that takes time and instruction to improve.

With very young students, emphasis can focus on simply making letters clear. After all, letters and word formation are the starting blocks of written language. The next phase in development can focus on actually creating words and making sure they are spelled correctly. When students are at the sentence development stage, grammar and linguistic rules become a priority. The foundations of the English language need to be firm in order for students to have good writing. When students have progressed to more advanced levels and are composing fully formed sentences with a specific purpose, it's time to incorporate content-related feedback.

Feedback at all levels of writing development is crucial; this is how students will learn to correct mistakes and strengthen growing skills. Instructor feedback must be clear while also being sensitive to the students' struggles or backgrounds. Differentiated instruction may be required to bolster students' writing skills. A good starting point for overall writing instruction is to introduce students to the stages of writing an original piece.

The goal with the stages of writing is to build on the previous work. The prewriting stage is the time for students to just write down ideas and plan on how they will approach the topic at hand. The actual writing stage then dovetails on this fluidly because the student already has a framework of what the writing will focus on and how they will present information. In addition to practicing physical writing, these stages focus on critical thinking and planning skills and may lessen the student's stress before they write and receive feedback. Feedback on the initial writing, or first draft, is key. The instructor should be able to assess any difficulties and then steer the student toward improving their writing in the revision stage. After revisions, instructors should examine how effective their feedback was in helping the writing improve overall.

Methods of Feedback in the Writing Process

It is almost as important to provide feedback and evaluate a student's skill level as it is to teach. Most classes utilize both formative and summative assessments as a grading template. Although assessment and grading are not the same thing, assessments are often used to award a grade. A **formative assessment** monitors the student's progress in learning and allows continuous feedback throughout the course in the form of homework and in-class assignments, such as quizzes, writing workshops, conferences, or inquiry-based writing prompts. These assessments typically make up a lower percent of the overall grade. Alternatively, a **summative assessment** compares a student's progress in learning against some sort of standard, such as against the progress of other students or by the number of correct answers. These assessments usually make up a higher percent of the overall grade and come in the form of midterm or final exams, papers, or major projects.

One evidence-based method used to assess a student's progress is a rubric. A **rubric** is an evaluation tool that explicitly states the expectations of the assignment and breaks it down into different components. Each component has a clear description and relationship to the assignment as a whole. For writing, rubrics may be **holistic**, judging the overall quality of the writing, or they can be **analytic**, in which different aspects of the writing are evaluated (e.g., structure, style, word choices, and punctuation).

Rubrics can be used in all aspects of a curriculum, including reading comprehension, oral presentations, speeches, performances, papers, projects, and listening comprehension. They are usually formative in nature but can be summative depending on the purpose. Rubrics allow instructors to provide specific feedback and allow students to understand the expectations for an assignment.

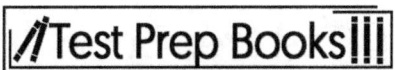

An example of an analytic rubric is displayed below:

Name _____ Date _____

Essay Rubric	4 Mastery	3 Satisfactory	2 Needs Improvement	1 Poor
Writing Quality	-Excellent usage of voice and style -Outstanding organizational skills -Wealth of relevant information	-Style and voice of essay was interesting -Mostly organized -Useful amount of information	-Inconsistent style and voice -Lacked clear organization -Small amount of useful information	-No noticeable style or voice -Virtually no organization -No relevant information
Grammar Conventions	-Essentially no mistakes in grammar -Correct spelling throughout	-Minor amount of grammar and spelling mistakes	-Many errors in grammar conventions and spelling	-Too many grammatical errors to understand the meaning of the piece

Another research-proven strategy is **conferencing**, in which students participate in a group discussion that usually involves the teacher. Students learn best when they can share their thoughts on what they've read or written and receive feedback from their peers and instructors. For writing, conferencing is frequently done in the revision stage. Through discussion, students are also able to enhance their listening and speaking skills. Conferences can be done in a one-on-one setting, typically between a student and instructor, or in a small group of students with guidance from the instructor. They are useful in that they provide an atmosphere of respect where a student can share their work and thoughts without fear of judgment. They increase motivation and allow students to explore a variety of topics and discussions. Conferences also allow the instructor to provide immediate feedback or prompt students for deeper explanations of their ideas. The most successful conferences have these characteristics:

- Have a set structure
- Focus on only a few points—too many are confusing or distracting
- Are solution based
- Allow students to both discuss their thoughts/works and receive/provide feedback for others
- Encourage the use of appropriate vocabulary
- Provide motivation and personal satisfaction or pleasure from reading and writing
- Allow a time where questions can be asked and immediately answered

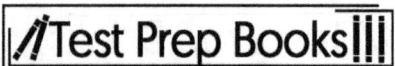

Rubrics and conferencing are both methods that provide useful feedback, one of the most important elements in the progress of a student's learning. **Feedback** is essentially corrective instruction delivered in writing, either verbally or non-verbally. Research has shown that the following techniques are the most effective when giving feedback.

Being Specific

For a student to know exactly how he or she is doing, feedback should be directed towards specific components of a student's writing, listening, or speaking skills, not a holistic overview. For example, writing "Excellent!" on a student's paper or homework is not useful information as it's unclear what was done well. A paper should provide useful comments throughout the body of the work, like saying "Wording is confusing here," or "Great use of adjectives." However, instructor comments should not overwhelm the student's writing; they should be used to focus their attention on specific areas of success or improvement. This encourages the student to keep doing what they are doing well and work on what needs improvement without being overwhelmed.

Being Sensitive

Giving feedback is precarious in nature as it entirely depends upon the emotional and mental states of the receiver. Some students do well with "tough love," while others may be discouraged and disheartened to see a slew of comments on their paper. Teachers should pay attention to how a student reacts to feedback. As a general rule, feedback should focus more on the positives so as not to damage self-esteem, while teaching students new techniques for self-correction, instead of simply criticizing what they've done. Also, it's important to try and be aware of the types of feedback each student responds the most effectively to, like providing oral feedback for students who don't read well.

Being Prompt

Feedback should be presented sooner rather than later, so that students will not have time to repeat mistakes they are unaware of that may become habitual. Studies have shown that students who are given immediate feedback display a greater increase in performance than those who were given feedback later in the term. As soon as the action has happened, it is important give the appropriate praise or critique so that the student associates the feedback with the action.

Being Explicit

It is important to explain the purpose of the feedback before it is given so that a student does not feel controlled, too closely examined, or competitive. This can cause the learner to feel self-conscious and discourage them from performing their best. The importance of feedback and how it is meant to improve on a personal skill set should be explained to the student.

Being Focused

Teachers should try and keep the feedback in alignment with the goal the student is expected to achieve. Too much feedback, especially if it is unrelated to the goal, can be overwhelming and distracting from the purpose of the assignment or paper.

Here are some other tips to consider when giving feedback:

- Teachers should be aware of their body language and facial expressions when giving feedback—a frown or grimace can be very discouraging, even if the written feedback was mostly positive.

- It's conducive to concentrate on one thing at a time. If a student submits a paper with a lot of errors, for example, it may be helpful to identify a prevalent pattern of error and work through strategies to correct it so that student does not feel overwhelmed.

- Using effective rubrics can make all the difference—letting students know exactly what is expected will provide them with a basis on which to model their techniques and skills.

- Students should be educated on giving feedback. This can be demonstrated by example and through instruction on how to give feedback in a positive, constructive way and correct any behavior that trends toward disrespect or excessive competition. Students should also provide feedback to the teacher as well.

- Teachers should not give the same comments to every student, but make them personal.

- When offering criticism, teachers should always offer tips for how the student can improve.

- It's important to avoid personal comments, e.g., "You're so smart!" or "Math isn't your best subject." Rather, the comments should focus on the writing: e.g., "The organization of this paper is clear."

- Students shouldn't be compared to each other, e.g., "Look how perfectly Victor composed this sentence!" This can galvanize the students into competing with one another.

High-Quality Writing

High-quality writing takes more than simply good writing skills and a knowledge of vocabulary. High-quality writing takes a lot of planning, writing, and revising in order to meet the standards of the audience. Many factors go into high-quality writing, but some major ones, including content, voice, and word choice, are listed below:

Content

The **content** of a piece of writing includes the ideas, structure, language, and effect of a particular text. Content begins with a writer being able to effectively brainstorm and research their topic in order to obtain credibility as an author. Thorough research of a topic and proper citation is the first step in creating good content. Organization of the text is also important to high-quality content, as is knowledge of vocabulary and sentence structure. Finally, good writing content will have an intended effect on the audience, whether that be persuading the audience to act or informing them of how something is done.

Voice

The voice an author selects is also important to note. An author's **voice** is that element of style that indicates their personality. It's important that authors move us as readers; therefore, they will choose a voice that helps them do that. An author's voice may be satirical or authoritative. It may be light-hearted or serious in tone. It may be silly or humorous as well. Voice, as an element of style, can be vague in nature and difficult to identify, since it's also referred to as an author's tone, but it is that element unique to the author. It is the author's "self." A reader can expect an author's voice to vary across literary genres. A non-fiction author will generally employ a more neutral voice than an author of fiction, but use caution when trying to identify voice. Do not confuse an author's voice with a particular character's voice.

Word Choice

An author's **word choice** helps to convey meaning in a particular way. Through diction, an author can convey a particular tone—e.g., a humorous tone, a serious tone—in order to support the thesis in a meaningful way to the reader.

Connotation

Connotation is when an author chooses words or phrases that invoke ideas or feelings other than their literal meaning. An example of the use of connotation is the word *cheap*, which suggests something is poor in value or negatively describes a person as reluctant to spend money. When something or someone is described this way, the reader is more inclined to have a particular image or feeling about it. Thus, connotation can be a very effective language tool in creating emotion and swaying opinion. However, connotations are sometimes hard to pin down because varying emotions can be associated with a word. Generally, though, connotative meanings tend to be fairly consistent within a specific cultural group.

Denotation

Denotation refers to an author's use of words or phrases to mean exactly what they say. It is helpful when a writer wants to present hard facts or vocabulary terms with which readers may be unfamiliar. Some examples of denotation are the words *inexpensive* and *frugal*. *Inexpensive* refers to the cost of something, not its value, and *frugal* indicates that a person is conscientiously watching their spending. These terms do not elicit the same emotions that *cheap* does.

Authors sometimes choose to use both, but what they choose and when they use it is what critical readers need to differentiate. One method isn't inherently better than the other; however, one may create a better effect, depending upon an author's intent. If, for example, an author's purpose is to inform, to instruct, and to familiarize readers with a difficult subject, their use of connotation may be helpful. However, it may also undermine credibility and confuse readers. An author who wants to create a credible, scholarly effect in their text would most likely use denotation, which emphasizes literal, factual meaning and examples.

Using Evidence-Based Practices to Motivate Learners

Making Reading Enjoyable

Teaching students *how* to read is one thing; training them to *enjoy* reading is another. Below are some strategies for encouraging reading in your classroom.

- Model the attitude toward reading that you would like to see in your students. Attitude is contagious; if you show your students that you enjoy reading, they will learn to be enthusiastic about it as well.

- Create activities that allow students to choose which book they will read. Selecting their own books gives students a sense of agency, which in turn makes them more engaged in their reading.

- Recommend books to individual students. If your student mentions a topic that interests them, recommend a book about the issue. When teaching on a subject, you can also accompany assigned reading with suggested reading for students who are interested in the topic and want to learn more about it.

- Do not allow students to struggle too much. If reading becomes an immensely frustrating experience, students will avoid it. You can prevent this problem by selecting appropriately complex material for your students and giving struggling readers extra help.

- Create a class environment where reading is a positive activity. Do not call students negative names like "nerd" when they read; discourage other students from using them. Praising students for reading is also helpful.

- Read aloud to your students, and encourage parents to do the same. Listening enables students to enjoy literature that is above their reading level. Reading aloud is particularly important for young students who cannot yet read interesting material by themselves, and it promotes a positive attitude toward reading in students of all ages.

- Encourage students to read at home, not just at school. Reading challenges can be useful, particularly over school breaks.

Incorporating Technology to Encourage Student-Centered Learning

Using Technology in Reading Lessons

Technology can be a useful tool in the classroom, but teachers must be careful when integrating it into lessons.

Teach your students how to evaluate material from the internet. Just as teachers need to be aware that some online resources are unreliable, students should learn to recognize high quality and low quality material. Students of all ages can learn age-appropriate lessons about source reliability. For example, you might teach younger students that not every source is reliable by showing them how anyone can edit Wikipedia articles. Evaluating sources is particularly important for older students who are beginning to write research essays. These students can learn the same criteria as teachers use for evaluating research. It may be helpful to go through sources as a class and discuss whether they are reliable.

Be aware that your students will have different degrees of technological literacy. **Technological literacy** refers to a student's ability to use electronic devices. For example, a student who knows how to use computers and can easily navigate the internet has high technological literacy; a student who struggles to use electronic devices, on the other hand, has low technological literacy. Children's technological literacy largely depends on their home environment. Some families have computers and allow the students to use them; some students have their own computers; and some lack access altogether. Therefore, you will need to observe each student and offer help to those who are struggling.

Set up parameters to ensure that students' interactions with technology are educational, not distracting. For example, a teacher who is having their students practice writing on a tablet app should ensure that the tablets are locked and will not allow students to exit the app. Otherwise, students will probably waste time playing games instead of practicing their writing.

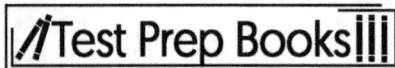

Student-Centered Learning

Teachers should strive to further student-centered learning. **Student-centered learning** (also known as **learner-centered education**) refers to educational practices that allow students to make choices about how or what they will learn. For example, a teacher who allows students to write essays on subjects that interest them instead of assigning a topic is practicing student-centered learning. Teachers who use this approach may also allow students to be involved in choosing the details of what they learn (such as which book the class will read) and the methods by which they will be assessed (such as whether they will be assigned a test, a presentation, or an essay). Here are some instructional methods that further this approach.

Ask guiding questions instead of providing answers. Asking questions motivates students to be curious and explore the material for themselves instead of just memorizing facts. For example, a teacher who begins a lesson by listing out characteristics of poetry is only teaching their students facts, while a teacher who asks students to think of factors that differentiate poetry and prose is engaging students' critical thinking skills and teaching them to think independently.

Break students into small groups for discussion or activities. For example, a teacher might divide students into groups and have each discuss a different aspect of a novel. After these discussions, each group would give a short presentation to the rest of the class and explain their thoughts.

Give students options, both in learning and evaluation. For example, a teacher could allow students to guide their own learning by giving them time for independent reading. In a similar way, a teacher could let students choose whether they want to give a presentation or create a poster: this choice would allow students to select a format that interests them and caters to their strengths.

Finally, teachers should work to build information-rich classrooms.

Information-Rich Environment

An **information-rich environment** is a setting that makes it easy for students to access information in a variety of ways. For example, a classroom where there are few books and few independent learning activities is not information-rich. An information-rich classroom, on the other hand, includes a variety of books that appeal to students with different interests, as well as activities designed to engage students. There are countless ways to make your classroom more information-rich; below are some ideas to get you started.

Build a rich classroom library. There should be plenty of books, and you should feature a variety of topics so that students with different interests are engaged. Classroom libraries are also a great place to include multicultural and diverse literature, as doing so will help minority students feel included and spark others' interest in learning about new cultures.

Integrate technology into your classroom. Computers and tablets can help students who have high technological literacy but are not interested in reading engage with the material. For example, a student who plays video games at home but thinks reading is nerdy may be more motivated to read on a device. Technology can also make your material more accessible to children with special needs, as many children who are on the autism spectrum or have other conditions feel overstimulated by in-person contact and prefer to interact with devices.

Learning Environments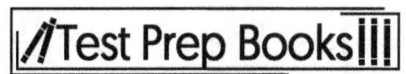

Use your wall space. Empty walls create an unwelcoming environment that is not conducive to learning. Walls are an excellent space to create collaborative posters about the material your students are learning, put up charts that will help your students learn new information, and display student work.

Organizational Structures and Classroom Management Practices

Planning Differentiated Reading Instruction

The following are key factors to consider in planning differentiated reading instruction:

- Assess knowledge and skills in the specific area(s) of reading.
  - Identify the prerequisite skills that are required for students to benefit from instruction.
  - Properly pace the instruction of such skills.
  - Understand the complexity of the skills and content that should be presented.
  - Provide scaffolding to ensure that all students can access higher-level reading knowledge and skills.

The breakdown of materials and standards over a week is vital. A weeklong reading lesson can be broken down into five sections or days. Skills presented throughout the course of the lesson can be assessed at the end of the week. Teachers can evaluate student advancement more effectively with smaller group sizes. Therefore, initial assessments should be used to differentiate instruction and to group students according to their abilities and skill levels. Students who have mastered the skill(s) can move at a faster pace and on to more complex tasks while working at their seat independently. This gives the instructor time to meet with students who need more remediation and teacher direction. Students who need the most help should meet with the teacher individually for scaffolded remediation of less-complex tasks. Struggling students also benefit from slower-paced lessons and additional practice.

The anchor standards for college and career readiness include key ideas and details, craft and structure, and integration of knowledge and ideas:

- **Ideas and details:** Students must be able to make inferences and draw conclusions from a text, determine central ideas and themes, and analyze how authors develop individuals, events, and ideas throughout the text.

- **Craft and structure:** Students will need to interpret figurative meanings, analyze how parts of a text relate to each other, and assess points of view.

- **Integration of knowledge and ideas:** Students must evaluate content across a variety of media and formats.

Meeting the Needs of all Students

The following are ways for educators to organize and manage differentiated reading instruction and interventions to meet the needs of all students:

- Use flexible grouping, individualized instruction, and whole-class instruction as needed.

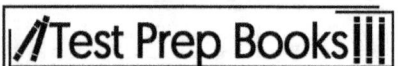

- Use all components of their state's adopted materials to make grade-level content accessible for all students.
- Create intervention groups according to the severity of student needs.

Reading instruction begins with daily whole-class lessons that are conducted to introduce new skills. The remaining time of a reading lesson should be dedicated to independent practice for those who have mastered the skill and intervention time for students who are progressing towards the skill.

Lessons should utilize materials adopted by the practitioner's own state. These materials have been evaluated for consistency with the state's standards and benchmarks. Materials that have been evaluated by one's own state include textbooks, technology-based resources, curriculum sets, and tests. Thus, there are enough materials to use with all types of learners to ensure accessibility for all students.

Students should be assessed during daily lessons. Formative assessments can be done on a daily basis through informal observations. Summative assessments can be done weekly. The teacher ought to use student performance on such assessments to organize the students into smaller intervention groups. The organization of such groups helps to ensure that all students are provided with differentiated interventions on the exact skills in which they struggle. Students who display difficulty in a skill should meet with a teacher for one-on-one or small-group remediation more frequently than students who have mastered the skill. These latter students will be given more independent work at their seats. Groups can be changed accordingly as students' performance changes.

Evidence-Based Intervention for Learners Who Have Not Mastered Grade-Level Standards

Helping Students Who Read Below Grade Level

In any classroom, there will be students who fall behind or are at risk for struggling in the future. Here are some ways to recognize these students, preventing failure before it happens and helping students who are behind get back on track.

Implement screening assessments at the start of the school year. For example, you might administer the Informal Reading Inventory during the first few weeks of class to determine whether any of your students are at risk and would benefit from intervention.

Build communication with your students' parents, and suggest ways for parents of at-risk students to improve their children's performance, such as reading with them or supervising their homework. Often, parents who know that their child is struggling at school can take steps to help the student work through these issues at home before they become a bigger problem. For example, telling a couple that their son is performing poorly on spelling tests might enable the parents to motivate their child to practice at home and catch up with the rest of the class.

Make sure that at-risk students are receiving adequate peer support. **Peer support** is the help that students receive from other students. For example, if a struggling student asks another student to explain something, they are asking for peer support. Peer support is important because it increases the engagement in your classroom and builds a sense of community and responsibility. You can encourage students to help each other by seating at-risk students near high performers, implementing a buddy system, and breaking students into groups.

Scaffolding is a method of making students' workload seem less overwhelming by dividing it into manageable sections. Instead of assigning all the work at once and letting students either accomplish it or fail, teachers break the learning into steps and help students accomplish each one. For example, a teacher might scaffold by teaching the unfamiliar vocabulary in a text before the students read it. Scaffolding is a great way of preventing confusion and helping students with poor organization skills stay on track.

Multisensory instruction is a method of integrating touch, sight, and hearing to teach new skills. For example, a teacher might have a student draw new vocabulary words after reading them or hearing them. By appealing to multiple areas of the brain, multisensory instruction builds strong memory cues and puts students with different strengths (for example, visual learners and auditory learners) on an equal playing field.

Practice Quiz

1. A teacher is planning to introduce new material to students regarding a complex topic in writing. Which of the following would be the best method for the teacher to use?
    a. Flexible grouping
    b. Student-based grouping
    c. No grouping
    d. Teacher-based grouping

2. The value of writing a reading response is primarily which of the following?
    a. Improving reading comprehension
    b. Learning to react to texts
    c. Learning to answer text-driven questions
    d. Practicing their own writing skills

3. Differentiated instruction, especially in terms of reading and writing, refers to which of the following?
    a. Breaking students into different groups based on language levels
    b. Varied teaching methods that lead to equity in language acquisition
    c. Different teachers reinforcing the same topic to speed learning
    d. Providing different types of literature to improve comprehension

See answers on the next page.

Answer Explanations

1. D: In teacher-based grouping, the teacher maintains more control over the direction of learners and is better able to facilitate understanding by providing differentiating instruction as needed. Choice A is incorrect because it includes both teacher- and student-based groupings, and for complex or new material, student groups may easily confuse or mislead one another on key concepts. For that reason, student-based learning should be used when students understand concepts well enough to work within their groups or independently. Choice B is also incorrect because student-based grouping is more hands-off for the teacher, and although it allows students to learn from one another, they need direct instruction on key concepts for new or complex ideas. Choice C is incorrect; although independent learning is an option, when it comes to understanding the concepts discussed in writing, students are more successful working in groups or with partners.

2. A: A reading response asks students to read a text and then write about their reactions or draw conclusions about the text. Students improve their comprehension skills by practicing understanding what a text is saying as well as what a text means or how it connects to the world. Choice B is incorrect because students do not necessarily need to be taught how to react to a text. Although asking questions may help them explore their reactions, learning to answer a question is not the end goal, so Choice C is incorrect. Finally, although it does allow them to practice their writing skills, Choice D, the primary goal is comprehension, and writing is a strategy that helps them achieve the primary goal rather than it being the goal itself.

3. B: Differentiated instruction means tailoring lessons, exercises, and classroom activities to meet the needs of individual learners to assist them all in gaining the language skills they need to be successful. Breaking students into groups, Choice A, may be useful in a classroom for certain tasks, but student-based groups may not provide varied instructions, and even within a group at the same level, learning needs are different. Choice C is incorrect because differentiated instruction is something a skilled individual teacher should be able to provide to students on their own. Finally, because differentiation does not have to do with types of literature but perhaps the varied ways a teacher would teach those texts to different students, Choice D is incorrect.

Oral and Written Language Acquisition

Oral Language Acquisition Concepts

Instructional Strategies for Oral Language, Listening and Speaking Skills, and Vocabularies

Oral or spoken language is important when understanding a text. If proficient, a reader's speech will aid their ability to understand and comprehend words, sentences, paragraphs, and a variety of complex texts.

Oral language activities, such as purposeful read-alouds, allow students to focus on comprehension skills. Listening skills can promote and serve as a great foundation for comprehension skills. Understanding a text advances students' comprehension skills. When an instructor reads aloud, a student does not need to decode words for fluency. This allows students to listen and focus solely on the text for comprehension. Teacher read-alouds also provide students the opportunity to learn how to emphasize voice and tone while reading.

Learning of Standard American English by Speakers of Other Languages

Inevitably, all languages deviate from their standard format. In America, Standard American English has evolved into different forms, or **dialects**, that are spoken across the country based on cultural influences and location. These dialects, while still considered English, are not Standard English. This is because some of the grammar, pronunciations, or general phonetics are inconsistent with the designated standard. Whether students are native English speakers or learning English as a second language, learning Standard English will give them a holistic understanding of American language conventions.

Students have likely encountered examples of American English deviation before, so the risk here is that they think slang or idiomatic choices reflect correct English usage. It's important to frequently review English language structure to ensure students know the proper pronunciations of words and how sentences fit together. However, this still doesn't eliminate confusion with hearing other English dialects; after all, these dialects are still English. One way to teach students Standard American English is to illustrate the difference between the standard and other dialects.

Citing specific examples of dialectic English that are incorrect from the standard is key. For example, Americans living in the South tend to use the word *y'all* to summarize the phrase *you all*. *Y'all* isn't recognized as part of Standard American English, so the correct version is *you all*. Distinctions such as this will help students visualize and hear proper English in use, which will help them recognize and use Standard English when reading and speaking.

In addition to reviewing proper word use and phonetics, training should also incorporate pronunciation. Writing and reading Standard English is very important, but students should also be knowledgeable of the incorrect and correct way to say the words they're reading. In addition to explaining pronunciation rules, instructors can periodically ask students to say and pronounce random words in a reading passage to test their skills. Again, showing students correct and incorrect pronunciations will build their familiarity with correct Standard English and help them distinguish wrong pronunciation tropes. Visualization activities and tools will also help. Flash cards with pronunciation guides for keywords are just one way to help students pronounce difficult vocabulary words.

Relationship Between Language Acquisition and Students with Disorders

The **Nativist theory of language development** holds that humans learn speech naturally as a result of inborn ability. According to the theory, children naturally have a language acquisition device that enables them to understand and eventually replicate the language. Children are naturally inclined to pick up language. However, this view can be seen as contrary to the **interactionist learning view**, which holds that children learn language as a result of their interaction with others. Therefore, the more children are exposed to language, the more they pick up vocabulary and can string together phrases. It's helpful and open-minded to consider that both ideas impact language learning.

An instructor can assess students to see if their issues are based on lack of instruction or erroneous exposure to language or if a student has a learning disorder that is inhibiting their ability to learn as fluidly as other students. There are several language-related disorders and delays that could be making reading difficult for students, so identifying these issues early is key.

Instructors must be patient and engaging to assess student performance and encourage them to not fear failure. Hearing how students respond to reading or actually speak will give indications of what issues are present. For example, students who face difficulties with written English by reversing words or letters and sometimes having trouble identifying rhyming words may have common dyslexia. Another common problem is difficulty recognizing letter sounds, which delays students' language progression. All of these issues may occur naturally, interrupting learning ability, but they can be treated through differentiated instruction.

The most effective way to remedy language issues is to identify specific areas of difficulties and provide supplemental instruction. This process is referred to as **articulation therapy**. The first step is isolation, to see if students can make key sounds or help them make the sounds needed for English. Instructors then work to improve the students' understanding of syllables, words, phrases, sentences, reading, and conversation. All of these areas build on each other. Improving English sound production will impact the understanding of syllables and words and therefore pave the way for reading and speaking proficiency.

Linguistic and Cultural Diversity

The classroom must be a place that emphasizes respect for all individuals as well as collaboration to achieve a successful learning environment. In addition to teaching reading skills, the instructor is expected to be a model of tolerance and inclusiveness for all students, thus encouraging them to be open-minded toward others. In the United States, it's likely that instructors will have students from a broad range of cultural and linguistic backgrounds. Obviously, these students must be made to feel welcome, and any linguistic difficulties they have should be treated as simply another step in the learning process, not a result of their background. Any difficulty is an opportunity for the whole class to learn and grow.

Encouraging polite and respectful behavior is key. An instructor doesn't necessarily need to explain polite behavior, but rather, should serve as a role model for the class. When addressing students' issues, the teacher should be sensitive to how they feel and be encouraging no matter their religious or ethnic background. It's also important to monitor how students act and respond to one another. Proper language and behavior should be enforced when necessary, and if there is ever anything rude or insensitive said or done, it must be addressed and corrected. Teachers should emphasize the idea that, while everyone is different, they are all equal. Therefore, students must be treated respectfully. Teachers should observe whether students are listening to other students and not being distracted or

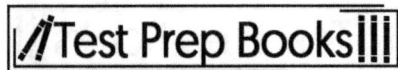

showing signs of disrespect. Tone and physical behavior must also be monitored; there's no excuse for rudeness. When disrespect occurs, steps should be taken to ensure it isn't repeated. It's important to remember that behaviors and lessons in early learners will inform how children grow and mature.

Reading and writing activities can also provide lessons in respect and collaboration. For instance, students can do group work on a text that discusses respectful behavior for reading practice, and also talk about the meaning of the written content. Other lessons can look at readings from different cultures to expand the students' appreciation and interest in diversity.

Written Language Acquisition Concepts

Vocabulary knowledge is an indicator and predictor of comprehension. If students find a match between a word within a text and a word that they've learned through listening and speaking, they are likelier to recognize and understand the meaning of the word in the written context. As the students will spend less time decoding and interpreting the word, they are likelier to read fluently and with comprehension. In contrast, if students cannot connect a written word to a word within their speaking or listening vocabulary, their fluency and comprehension may be interrupted. This proves to be true even if the student is able to correctly pronounce the word.

Reading Multisyllabic Words

Reading competence of multisyllabic words is accomplished through phonics skills that are accompanied by a reader's ability to recognize morphological structures within words. **Structural analysis** is a word recognition skill that focuses on the meanings of word parts, or morphemes, during the introduction of a new word. Therefore, the instruction of structural analysis focuses on the recognition and application of morphemes. **Morphemes** are word parts such as base words, prefixes, inflections, and suffixes. Students can use structural analysis skills to find familiar word parts within an unfamiliar word in order to decode the word and determine the definition of the new word. Identification and association of such word segments also aids the proper pronunciation and spelling of new multisyllabic words.

Similarly, learning to use phonics skills with more difficult words depends on a reader's ability to notice syllable structures within words that have more than one syllable. **Syllabic analysis**, or **syllabication**, is a skill that teaches students how to analyze words and separate them into syllables. **Syllables** are phonological units that contain a vowel sound. Teaching students how to break apart multisyllabic words into morphological and phonological units can greatly help them not to be intimidated by long words, since these tools will help them use syllable types to make longer words seem like a series of smaller words. The identified syllables can then be blended, pronounced, and/or written together as a single word. This helps students learn to decode and encode the longer words more accurately and efficiently with less anxiety. Thus, syllabic analysis leads to the rapid word recognition that is critical in reading fluency and comprehension.

Oral and Written Language Acquisition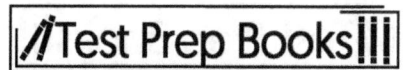

The following table identifies the six basic syllable patterns that should be explicitly taught during syllabic instruction:

Basic Syllable Patterns		
Name of Syllable Type	Characteristics of Syllable Type	Examples
Closed	A syllable with a single vowel closed in by a consonant.	lab, bog, an
Open	A syllable that ends with a single vowel. Note that the letter *y* acts as a vowel.	go, me, sly
Vowel-Consonant-Silent *e*	A syllable with a single vowel followed by a consonant then *e*.	like, rake, note, obese
Vowel Teams	A syllable that has two consecutive vowels. Note that the letters *w* and *y* act as vowels.	meat, pertain, bay, toad, window
R-controlled	A syllable with one or two vowels followed by the letter *r*.	car, jar, fir, sir, collar, turmoil
Consonant *le* (-*al*, -*el*) Also called final stable	A syllable that has a consonant followed by the letters *le*, *al*, or *el*.	puddle, stable, uncle, bridal, pedal
Other final stable syllables	A syllable at the end of words can be taught as a recognizable unit such as *cious*, *age*, *ture*, *tion*, or *sion*.	pension, elation, puncture, stumpage, fictitious

Practices for Developing Students' Reading and Writing Skills

Sight Word Instruction

The goal of **sight word instruction** is to help students readily recognize regular and irregular high-frequency words in order to aid reading fluency and comprehension. Several factors affect the sequence of instruction for specific sight words. For example, before a child is exposed to sight words, he or she needs to be able to fluently recognize and say the sound of all uppercase and lowercase letters. Also, students need to be able to accurately decode target words before they recognize sight words. When

Oral and Written Language Acquisition

irregular words are introduced, attention should be drawn to both the phonetically regular and the phonetically irregular portions of the words.

Before sight word instruction can begin, teachers need to identify high-frequency words that do and do not follow normal spelling conventions, but are used often. Teachers may choose to select words that are used often within their students' reading materials, words that students have an interest in learning, or content-specific words. Alternatively, grade-level standardized sight word lists, such as the Dolch word lists, can be referenced.

Sight Word Activities

Repetition and exposure through guided and independent practice are essential in student retention of sight words. Each lesson should introduce only three to five new sight words and also review words from previous lessons. Visually similar words should not be introduced in proximity to one another. Sample activities through which sight words can be taught are listed below.

- Students can practice reading decodable texts and word lists.

- Teachers should read text that contains the sight words that a class is currently learning. As a teacher reads aloud, they should pause, point to, and correctly pronounce the words. Instead of pointing to the words, teachers can underline or highlight the words as they appear in sentences that are read.

- Flashcards can be used to practice sight word recognition.

- Games are fun and motivating avenues through which sight words can be practiced. Examples of games that can be used to practice sight words include Bingo, Go Fish, and Memory.

- As students learn new sight words, they can write them in a sight word "dictionary." Students should be asked to write a sentence using each sight word included within the dictionary.

High-Frequency Sight Word Activities

The spelling of high-frequency words should be taught after students have been exposed to the words, can readily recognize the words, and can read the words. The following multisensory strategies can be used to help students master the spelling of high-frequency sight words.

- Spell reading: Spell reading begins when a student says the high-frequency word. Then, the student spells out the letters in the word. Lastly, the student reads the word again. Spell reading helps commit the word to a student's memory when done in repetition.

- Air writing: When air writing, a student uses their finger to write the letters of a word in the air.

- Arm tapping: During arm tapping, a student says the word, spells the word's letters on their arm, and then reads the word again.

- **Table writing**: Students write the word on the table. A substrate, where the word is written in sand or shaving cream, can be added to the table.

- **Letter magnet spelling**: Arranging letter magnets on a metal surface, such as a cookie sheet, is a fun way for students to learn how to spell sight words. Because this strategy is seen as a game to the student, letter magnet spelling increases student motivation to write words.

- **Material writing**: Students can use clay, play dough, Wikki sticks, or other materials to form letters that are used to spell the words.

Developing Narrative, Argumentative, and Expository Writing

Writing can be classified under three passage types: narrative, expository, and argumentative. Though these types are not mutually exclusive, one form tends to dominate the rest. By recognizing the *type* of passage you're reading, you gain insight into *how* you should read. If you're reading a narrative, you can assume the author intends to entertain, which means you may skim the text without losing meaning. An argumentative essay might require a close read because skimming the passage might cause the reader to miss salient details.

1. *Narrative* writing, at its core, is the art of storytelling. For a narrative to exist, certain elements must be present. First, it must have characters. While many characters are human, characters could be defined as anything that thinks, acts, and talks like a human. For example, many recent movies, such as *Lord of the Rings* and *The Chronicles of Narnia*, include animals, fantastical creatures, and even trees that behave like humans. Second, it must have a plot or sequence of events. Typically, those events follow a standard plot diagram, but recent trends start *in medias res* or in the middle (near the climax). In this instance, foreshadowing and flashbacks often fill in plot details. Finally, along with characters and a plot, there must also be conflict. Conflict is usually divided into two types: internal and external. Internal conflict indicates the character is in turmoil and is presented through the character's thoughts.

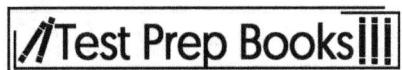

Oral and Written Language Acquisition

External conflicts are visible. Types of external conflict include a person versus nature, another person, or society.

2. *Expository* writing is detached and to the point, while other types of writing—persuasive, narrative, and descriptive—are lively. Since expository writing is designed to instruct or inform, it usually involves directions and steps written in second person ("you" voice) and lacks any persuasive or narrative elements. Sequence words such as *first*, *second*, and *third*, or *in the first place*, *secondly*, and *lastly* are often given to add fluency and cohesion. Common examples of expository writing include instructor's lessons, cookbook recipes, and repair manuals.

3. *Argumentative* writing requires writers to research a topic and take a position on it while backing their stance with evidence. The topic, stance, and arguments are found in the thesis, positioned near the end of the introduction. Later supporting paragraphs offer relevant quotations, paraphrases, and summaries from primary or secondary sources, which are then interpreted, analyzed, and evaluated. The goal of argumentative writers is not to stack quotes but to develop original ideas by using sources as a starting point. Good argumentative writing makes powerful arguments with valid sources and thoughtful analysis. Poor argumentative writing is riddled with bias and logical fallacies. Sometimes logical and illogical arguments are sandwiched together in the same piece. This is to be avoided when developing an argumentative essay.

Writing as a Developmental Process

Almost all coherent written works contain three primary parts: a beginning, middle, and end. The organizational arrangements differ widely across distinct writing modes. Argumentative and expository texts utilize an introduction, body, and conclusion whereas narrative works use an orientation, series of events/conflict, and a resolution.

Every element within a written piece relates back to the main idea, and the beginning of a persuasive or expository text generally conveys the main idea or the purpose. For a narrative piece, the beginning is the section that acquaints the reader with the characters and setting, directing them to the purpose of the writing. The main idea in narrative may be implied or addressed at the end of the piece.

Depending on the primary purpose, the arrangement of the middle will adhere to one of the basic organizational structures described in the information texts and rhetoric section. They are cause and effect, problem and solution, compare and contrast, description/spatial, sequence, and order of importance.

The ending of a text is the metaphorical wrap-up of the writing. A solid ending is crucial for effective writing as it ties together loose ends, resolves the action, highlights the main points, or repeats the

Oral and Written Language Acquisition

central idea. A **conclusion** ensures that readers come away from a text understanding the author's main idea. The table below highlights the important characteristics of each part of a piece of writing.

Structure	Argumentative/Informative	Narrative
Beginning	Introduction Purpose, main idea	Orientation Introduces characters, setting, necessary background
Middle	Body Supporting details, reasons, and evidence	Events/Conflict Story's events that revolve around a central conflict
End	Conclusion Highlights main points, summarizes and paraphrases ideas, reiterates the main idea	Resolution The solving of the central conflict

Oral and Written Communication, Phonological Awareness, Print Concepts, Alphabet Knowledge, Decoding, Fluency, Vocabulary, and Comprehension

Building Oral Communication Skills

Oral language and presentation are also important in learning reading comprehension. Reviewing and identifying new and key vocabulary prior to reading the text helps students understand the text more efficiently. Once students are familiar with new vocabulary words, they will understand the paragraph with a new key word when approaching it, rather than reaching the word and skipping over the true meaning of the sentence or paragraph at large, or needing to stop and look up the word before continuing to read. This interrupts fluency as well as the understanding of the text. Previewing text and skimming pictures for younger students, or reviewing bold subtitles for older students, can benefit students' comprehension by helping to gain an idea of what the text may be about before reading. There are different ways to find a text's purpose using auditory and speech skills, some of which include summarizing with a peer or paraphrasing the text.

When students are paired together or placed in small groups, they can share and discuss elements of texts. Literature circles are like book clubs. These circles allow students to speak freely, create their own discussions, and form questions about the text. Teachers can provide literature circle booklets, which may contain response or discussion questions to enhance conversation within the group.

Oral and Nonverbal Communication Skills in Various Settings
Early childhood educators are instrumental in developing effective communication skills in their students. Verbal and nonverbal communication skills are important in setting a positive, educational,

supportive environment to optimize learning. They are equally important for students to master for use in their own daily lives. When communicating with others, students should be mindful to be fully attentive, make eye contact, and use encouraging facial expressions and body language to augment positive verbal feedback. Postures including hands on hips or crossed over the chest may appear standoffish, while smiling and nodding enhance the comfort and satisfaction of the other party. Active listening is the process of trying to understand the underlying meaning in someone else's words, which builds empathy and trust. Asking open-ended questions and repeating or rephrasing in a reflective or clarifying manner is a form of active listening that builds a positive, trusting relationship.

In tandem with different communication styles, educators and students alike should be aware of different learning styles. **Auditory learners** learn through hearing, so the educator can use verbal descriptions and instructions. **Visual learners** learn through observation, so the educator can use demonstrations, provide written and pictorial instructional content, and show videos. **Kinesthetic learners** learn through movement, involvement, and experience, so the educator can prepare lessons with hands-on learning, labs, or games with a physical component.

An important skill for children is the ability to communicate effectively with adults, and developing this comfort from a young age will be helpful throughout life. Educators can facilitate this through providing experiences where children need to talk to adults in the community. For example, educators may take the class on a field trip to the local community library, where students must ask the librarian for help locating certain health resources. Students might also prepare a health fair and invite parents, community members, and those from senior centers to come learn from posters, demonstrations, and presentations. Children can also work on developing communication skills using an array of technologies such as telephone, written word, email, and face-to-face communication.

Oral Language Structures

Oral language skills are important for students to have in order to thrive in an English-speaking environment. Beyond comprehending spoken English, understanding oral language structure helps students comprehend the context of what they are reading and how to respond appropriately. All languages utilize grammar, vocabulary, phonology, morphology, discourse, and pragmatics; these concepts combine to make words on a page actually form communication—the foundation of sentences.

As an instructor, it's important to be mindful of how comfortable the class is with oral language. Native speakers may be more proficient than those who are learning English as a second language; the latter may need more differentiated instruction to build their conceptual knowledge. No matter the range of student experiences, reading instructors should incorporate drills and lessons that frequently review oral language components throughout the course. This will ensure that core skills such as grammar and word formation remain fresh in students' minds as they continue to progress in reading proficiency. This can be done in a variety of ways and activities using both teacher-based and student-based grouping instruction.

Strategically, it's best to promote oral language by having students isolate and identify different aspects of sentences such as grammar and even vocabulary terms. Reviewing **phonology**, the sounds of English, and **morphology**, how words are formed, is also important. One way to review these aspects would be to present a sample of text and then have students deconstruct the sentences to identify these structures.

Discourse, which studies how language is used in communication, and **pragmatics**, which reflects the correct use of the language, can be reviewed through text examination and interactive activities. It's important to alter and differentiate instruction to review reading principles in different ways and expand critical thinking skills. One method for reviewing discourse and pragmatics would be for the instructor to write or speak a sentence and then have the class discuss the discourse and pragmatics together. Students can also create the sentences themselves, demonstrating their ability to replicate correct language structure and recognize incorrect sentence components. When reviewing language structure, instructors should continue to assess how students are grasping the material and monitor progress. It's important to remember that reading improvements begin with a strong understanding of language fundamentals.

Phonological Association Skills

Phonological awareness is the recognition that oral language is made of smaller units, such as syllables and words. Phonemic awareness is a type of phonological awareness. Phonemic-aware students recognize specific units of spoken language called phonemes. **Phonemes** are unique and easily identifiable units of sound. Examples include /t/, /b/, /c/, etc. It is through phonemes that words are distinguished from one another.

Phonemic Awareness in Reading Development

Phonological and phonemic awareness do not require written language because phonemic awareness is based entirely upon speech. However, phonological and phonemic awareness are the prerequisites for literacy. Thus, experts recommend that all kindergarten students develop phonemic awareness as part of their reading preparation.

Once students are able to recognize phonemes of spoken language, phonics can be implemented in grades K–2. Phonics is the direct correspondence between and blending of letters and sounds. Unlike phonemic awareness, **phonics** requires the presence of print. Phonics often begins with the alphabetic principle, which teaches that letters or other characters represent sounds. Students must be able to identify letters, symbols, and individual sounds before they can blend multiple sounds into word parts and whole words. Thus, phoneme awareness and phonics predict outcomes in word consciousness, vocabulary, reading, and spelling development.

Differentiating Instruction to Reach a Full Range of Learners

The following strategies can be used to develop phonological and phonemic awareness in students that struggle with reading, disabled learners, special-needs students, English Language Learners (ELLs), speakers of nonstandard English, and advanced learners:

- Differentiated instruction for struggling readers, disabled students, or students with special needs should include the re-teaching and/or emphasis of key skills, such as blending and segmenting. Such instruction should be supported through the employment of a variety of concrete examples that explain a concept or task. Teaching strategies of such concepts or tasks should utilize visual, kinesthetic, and tactile modalities, and ample practice time should be allotted.

- Instruction of phonological and phonemic awareness can also be differentiated for ELLs and speakers of nonstandard English. Most English phonemes are present in other languages. Therefore, teachers can capitalize on the transfer of relevant knowledge, skills, and phonemes

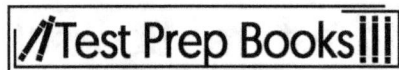

Oral and Written Language Acquisition

from a student's primary language into the English language. In this way, extra attention and instructional emphasis can be applied toward phonemes and phoneme sequences that are nontransferable between the two languages.

- Advanced learners benefit from phonological and phonemic instruction with greater breadth and depth. Such instruction should occur at a faster pace and expand students' current skills.

Continual Assessment of Phonological and Phonemic Awareness Needs to Occur

Entry-level assessments, progress monitoring, and summative assessments need to be administered in order to determine students' phonological and phonemic awareness. Appropriate formal and informal assessments for such purposes include:

The Yopp-Singer Test of Phonemic Segmentation

The **Yopp-Singer Test of Phonemic Segmentation** is an oral entry-level or summative assessment of phonemic awareness during which a teacher reads one of twenty-two words aloud at a time to a single student. The student is to break each word apart by stating the word's sounds in the order that the sounds are heard or said, and the teacher records the student's responses. Correctly segmented letter sounds are circled and incorrect responses are noted. If a student does well, then he or she is likely to do well in other phonemic areas. Upon poor student performance, the sound(s) with which a student struggles should be emphasized and/or retaught shortly after the time of the assessment.

After the Yopp-Singer Test, the blending of words, syllabification, and/or onset-rime identification should be assessed. The last set of phonological and phonemic skills to be assessed is composed of isolation, blending, deletion, and substitution.

Recognizing Rhyme Assessment

Word awareness, specifically awareness of onset-rime, can be assessed as a progress-monitoring activity. During the **recognizing rhyme assessment**, the teacher says two words. Students are to point their thumbs up if the words rhyme and down if the words do not rhyme. Immediate feedback and remediation are provided if the majority of the students respond incorrectly to a word pair.

Isolation or Matching Games

Games can be used to identify initial, medial, and final phonemes. During a **phoneme-isolation activity**, the teacher says one word at a time. The student is to tell the teacher the first, medial, or last sound of the word. During **phoneme-matching activities**, a teacher reads a group of words. The student is to say which two words from the group begin or end with the same sound. A similar activity can be completed to assess deletion and/or substitution (e.g., "What word would result if we replaced the /c/ of *cat* with an *h*?"). In this way, teachers can assess if remediation or extra instruction on initial, medial, or final phonemes is required, and lessons can be developed accordingly.

Phoneme Blending Assessment

In the **phoneme blending assessment**, a teacher says all the sounds within a word and a student listens to the teacher and is asked for the word that they hear when the sounds are put together quickly. This skill will be needed when students learn letter-sound pairs and decipher unknown words in their reading. Thus, mastery of this assessment can be used as an indicator to the teacher that the students are ready to learn higher-level phonological and/or phonemic tasks.

Please note that student results should be recorded, analyzed, and used to determine if students demonstrate mastery over the assessed skill and/or identify the needs of students. If mastery is not demonstrated, then the assessments should be used to determine exactly which letter-sound combinations or other phonemes need to be remediated. Any of the strategies earlier addressed (rhyming, blending, segmenting, deleting, substituting) can be used for such purposes.

Spelling as a Developmental Process

Decoding and encoding are reciprocal phonological skills, meaning that the steps to each are opposite of one another.

Decoding is the application of letter-sound correspondences, letter patterns, and other phonics relationships that help students read and correctly pronounce words. Decoding helps students to recognize and read words quickly, increasing reading fluency and comprehension. The order of the steps that occur during the decoding process are as follows:

1. The student identifies a written letter or letter combination.
2. The student makes correlations between the sound of the letter or sounds of the letter combination.
3. The student understands how the letters or letter combinations fit together.
4. The student verbally blends the letter and letter combinations together to form a word.

Encoding is the spelling of words. In order to properly spell words, students must be familiar with letter/sound correspondences. Students must be able to put together phonemes, digraphs or blends, morphological units, consonant/vowel patterns, etc. The steps of encoding are identified below:

1. The student understands that letters and sounds make up words.
2. The student segments the sound parts of a word.
3. The student identifies the letter or letter combinations that correspond to each sound part.
4. The student then writes the letters and letter combinations in order to create the word.

Because the stages of decoding and spelling are essentially opposite of one another, they are reciprocal skills. Thus, phonics knowledge supports the development of reading and spelling. Likewise, the development of spelling knowledge reinforces phonics and decoding knowledge. In fact, the foundation of all good spelling programs is their alignment to reading instruction and a student's reading level.

Because of the reciprocal relationship between decoding and encoding, the development of phonics, vocabulary, and spelling are interrelated. The instruction of phonics begins with simple syllable patterns. Phonics instruction then progresses toward more difficult syllable patterns, more complex phonics patterns, the sounds of morphemes, and strategies for decoding multisyllabic words. Through this process, new vocabulary is developed. Sight word instruction should not begin until students are able to decode target words with automaticity and accuracy. Spelling is the last instructional component to be introduced.

Spelling development occurs in stages. In order, these stages are the pre-phonetic stage, the semiphonetic stage, the phonetic stage, the transitional stage, and the conventional stage. Each stage is explained below. Ways in which phonics and vocabulary development fit into the spelling stages are discussed. Instructional strategies for each phase of spelling are suggested.

Spelling development begins with the **pre-phonetic stage**. This stage is marked by an incomplete understanding of the alphabetic principle. Student understanding of letter-sound correspondences is limited. During the pre-phonetic stage, students participate in precommunicative writing. **Precommunicative writing** appears to be a jumble of letter-like forms rather than a series of discrete letters. Students' precommunicative writing samples can be used as informal assessments of their understanding of the alphabetic principle and knowledge of letter-sound correspondences.

Pre-phonetic stage of spelling development

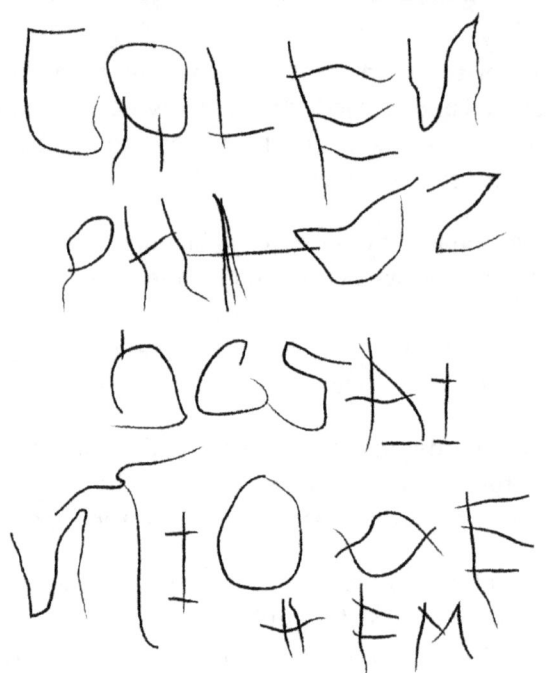

The pre-phonetic stage is followed by the **semiphonetic stage**. In this stage, a student understands that letters represent sounds. The alphabetic principle may be understood, but letter recognition may not yet be fully developed. In this stage, single letters may be used to represent entire words (e.g., *U* for *you*). Other times, multiple syllables within words may be omitted. Writing produced by students in this stage is still virtually unreadable. Teachers may ask students to provide drawings to supplement their writing to better determine what a student intended to write.

Semiphonetic stage of writing

The third stage in spelling development is the **phonetic stage**. In this stage, students have mastered letter-sound correspondences. Although letters may be written backward or upside down, phonetic spellers are able to write all of the letters in the alphabet. Because phonetic spellers have limited sight vocabulary, irregular words are often spelled incorrectly. However, words that are written may phonetically sound like the spoken word. Additionally, student writing becomes systematic. For example, students are likely to use one letter to represent a digraph or letter blend (e.g., *f* for /ph/).

Phonetic stage of writing

Spelling instruction of common consonant patterns, short vowel sounds, and common affixes or rimes can begin during the phonetic stage. Thus, spelling instruction during the phonetic stage coincides with the instruction of phonics and phonemic awareness that also occurs during this stage of development.

The creation of word walls is advantageous during the phonetic stage of spelling development. On a word wall, words that share common consonant-vowel patterns or letter clusters are written in groups. Students are encouraged to add words to the group. As a result, word walls promote strategic spelling, vocabulary development, common letter combinations, and common morphological units.

The **transitional stage** of spelling occurs when a student has developed a small sight vocabulary and a solid understanding of letter-sound correspondences. Thus, spelling dependence on phonology decreases. Instead, dependence on visual representation and word structure increases. As sight word vocabulary increases during the transition stage, the correct spelling of irregular words will also increase. However, students may still struggle to spell words with long vowel sounds.

Transitional stage of spelling

Differentiation of spelling instruction often begins during the transitional stage. Instruction ought to be guided by data collected through informal observations and informal assessments. Depending on individual needs, lessons may include sight word recognition, morphology, etymology, reading, and writing. It is during the transitional stage that the instruction of homophones can begin. **Homophones** are words that sound the same but have different spellings and meanings (e.g., *their* and *there*). Additionally, students should be expected to begin writing full sentences at the transitional stage. Writing will not only reinforce correct spelling of words but also phonics and vocabulary development.

Oral and Written Language Acquisition

Conventional spelling is the last and final stage of spelling development. This stage occurs after a student's sight word vocabulary recognition is well developed and the student is able to read fluently and with comprehension. By this stage, students know the basic rules of phonics. They are able to deal with consonants, multiple vowel-consonant blends, homophones, digraphs, and irregular spellings. Due to an increase in sight word recognition at this stage, a conventional speller is able to recognize when a word is spelled incorrectly.

It is at the conventional spelling stage that spelling instruction can begin to focus on content-specific vocabulary words and words with unusual spellings. In order to further reinforce vocabulary development of such content-specific words and apply phonic skills, students should be encouraged to use the correct spelling of such words within various writing activities.

For even the best conventional spellers, some words will still cause consistent trouble. Students can keep track of words that they consistently spell incorrectly or find confusing in word banks so they can isolate and eventually eliminate their individualized errors. Students can use their word banks as references when they come across a word with which they struggle. Students may also spend time consciously committing the words in their banks to memory through verbal or written practice.

Recognizing Common Orthographic Patterns

As students become more advanced in their decoding abilities, they will begin to read words that are increasingly more complex linguistically. Teachers should continue using decodable text so that students can continue practicing phonics elements and sight words already taught.

Whole-to-part instruction can be used with students who display more advanced decoding abilities. During whole-to-part instruction, a sentence, a word, and then a sound-symbol relationship is the focus of instruction. Additionally, CVCC, CCVC, and CVVC words that contain common and regular letter combinations can be taught as well as regular CVCe words. Teachers can begin introducing less common phonics elements, such as *kn* or *ph*. It is during this stage that students are taught how to add common inflected endings or suffixes (*-ed, -er, -est, -ing*, etc.) to single-syllable base words.

Finally, phonics knowledge is used to spell more complex orthographic patterns in single-syllable words. **Orthography** is the study of a language's spelling conventions. Orthography includes the rules of spelling, hyphenation, capitalization, pronunciation, emphasis, and word breaks. Orthographic processing requires students to use their visual systems to envision, store, recall, and form words. The prescribed teaching sequence of orthographic patterns is found in the next chart.

Orthographic Pattern	Example of Pattern
Awareness of letter-sound correspondences	Understanding that each letter has a certain sound as well as a name
Understanding that letters form words	Recoding certain CVC words like *dog, hug,* and *jar*
Simple consonant blends and matching sound patterns	Recognizing onsets and rimes of single-syllable words like *cat* as *c-at* and *star* as *st-ar*
Recognizing single-syllable words	Uses CVC, CCVC, or CVCC patterns
Ability to read more complex consonant blends	Reading and recognizing single-syllable words like *cross, lamp,* and *track*
Long versus short vowels	Identifying words that contain long and short vowel sounds
Vowel-Vowel and Vowel-Consonant Digraphs	Identifying words like *whey, tree,* and *phone*
Vowel-Vowel Digraphs that have the same sound	Identifying sounds such as /ay/, /ai/, or /a-e/
Vowel-Consonant Digraphs can be associated with different sounds	Identifying words like *cool* versus *boot, harm* versus *hare,* etc.
Complex single-syllable digraphs and trigraphs	Introducing the *tch* trigraph
Syllabication	Ability to split words into syllables
"Silent Letters" within words	Identifying words that contain silent letters such as *write, knock,* or *plumb*
Blending of two-syllable words	Reading two-syllable words such as *stumble, candle,* etc.
Morphemes within two-syllable words	Identifying correct syllabication of two-syllable words like *post-pone* versus *po-stpone*

Orthographic Pattern	Example of Pattern
Meaning of morphemes	An example would be knowing "macro" means "large" or "great"
Understanding letter clusters	Identifying that the "s" at the end of a word means its plural, and that the "ed" at the end of a word means it's in past tense.
Syllabication of nonconventional morphemes with multisyllabic words	Syllabication of morphemes that are not pronounced how they are written, like *ance* or *tion*.

Practice Quiz

1. Which of the following statements is true regarding decoding and encoding?
    a. Decoding is the spelling of words.
    b. Encoding helps students to recognize and read words quickly.
    c. Encoding is the application of letter-sound correspondences, letter patterns, and other phonics relationships.
    d. Decoding and encoding are learned in opposite stages or steps.

2. Which of the following is NOT true of word walls?
    a. They promote strategic spelling, vocabulary development, common letter combinations, and common morphological units.
    b. They help students sort words they know, want to know, and have learned.
    c. They are useful during the phonetic stage of spelling development.
    d. They group words that share common consonant-vowel patterns or letter clusters.

3. Which of the following INCORRECTLY matches the orthographic pattern with an example of the pattern?
    a. Vowel-vowel digraph that have the same sound: player and jail
    b. Vowel-vowel digraph that have the same sound: read and speed
    c. Vowel-consonant digraphs with different sounds: foot and fool
    d. Vowel-consonant digraphs with different sounds: harm and have

4. A local newspaper is looking for writers for a student column. A student would like to submit his article to the newspaper, but he isn't sure how to format his article according to journalistic standards. What resource should he use?
    a. A thesaurus
    b. A dictionary
    c. A style guide
    d. A grammar book

See answers on the next page.

Answer Explanations

1. D: Choice *D* is correct because decoding and encoding are reciprocal phonological skills, meaning that the steps to each are opposite of one another. It is because of this reciprocal relationship that the development of phonics, vocabulary, and spelling are interrelated. The other answer choices are incorrect because they ascribe the wrong term to the given definition or skill.

2. B: Word walls are a great tool for students as they learn to read, spell, and write. Because they help students pronounce unfamiliar words and have visual contact with the word along with the auditory experience, they are particularly useful in the phonetic stage of spelling development. All of the statements given are correct except Choice *B*, which describes KWL charts typically used for reading.

3. D: Choice *D* is an incorrect match between *harm* and *have*. These two words are vowel-constant digraphs that have the same sound.

4. C: A style guide offers advice about proper formatting, punctuation, and usage when writing for a specific field, such as journalism or scientific research. The other resources would not offer similar information. A dictionary is useful for looking up definitions; a thesaurus is useful for looking up synonyms and antonyms. A grammar book is useful for looking up specific grammar topics. Thus, Choices *A*, *B*, and *D* are incorrect.

Phonological Awareness

Phonological Awareness and Word Recognition Development

Concepts of Print and High-Frequency Sight Words

Print awareness aids reading development, as it is the understanding that the printed word represents the ideas voiced in spoken language. Print awareness includes the understanding that:

- Words are made of letters; spaces appear between words and words make sentences.
- Print is organized in a particular way (e.g., read from left to right and top to bottom, read from front to back, etc.), so books must be tracked and held accordingly.
- There are different types of print for different purposes (magazines, billboards, essays, fiction, etc.).

Print awareness provides the foundation on which all other literacy skills are built. It is often the first stage of reading development. Print awareness helps students develop skills such as word reading, reading comprehension, and letter-sound correspondence. For this reason, a child's performance on tasks relevant to their print awareness is indicative of the child's future reading achievement.

The following strategies can be used to increase print awareness in students:

- *An adult reads aloud to students and shared reading experiences.* In order to maximize print awareness within the student, the reader should point out the form, function, orientation, and sounds of letters and words.

- *Shared readings also build one-to-one correspondence.* **One-to-one correspondence** is the ability to match written letters or words to a spoken word when reading. This can be accomplished by pointing to words as they are read. This helps students make text-to-word connections. Pointing also aids **directionality**, or the ability to track the words that are being read.

- *Use the child's environment.* To reinforce print awareness, teachers can make a child aware of print in their environment, such as words on traffic signs. Teachers can reinforce this by labeling objects in the classroom.

- *Instruction of book organization can occur during read-alouds.* Students should be taught the proper orientation, tracking, and numbering conventions of books. For example, teachers can differentiate the title from the author's name on the front cover of a book.

- *Let students practice.* Allowing students to practice book-handling skills with wordless books, predictable text, or patterned text will help to instill print awareness.

Uppercase and Lowercase Letters

Among the skills that are used to determine reading readiness, letter identification is the strongest predictor. **Letter recognition** is the identification of each letter in the alphabet. Letter recognition does not include letter-sound correspondences; however, learning about and being able to recognize letters

Phonological Awareness

may increase student motivation to learn letter sounds. Also, the names of many letters are similar to their sounds, so letter recognition serves as a gateway for the letter-sound relationships that are needed for reading to occur. Similarly, the ability to differentiate between uppercase and lowercase letters is beneficial in determining where a sentence begins and ends.

To be fluent in letter identification, students should be able to identify letter names in and out of context with automaticity. In order to obtain such familiarity with the identification of letters, students need ample experience, acquaintance, and practice with letters. Explicit instruction in letter recognition, practice printing uppercase and lowercase letters of the alphabet, and consistent exposure to printed letters are essential in the instruction of letter recognition.

Research has revealed that the following sequencing guidelines are necessary to effectively promote letter naming and identification:

1. The initial stage includes visual discrimination of shapes and curved lines.

2. Once students are able to identify and discriminate shapes with ease, then letter formations can be introduced. During the introduction of letter shapes, two letters that share visual (*p* and *q*) or auditory (/a/ and /u/) similarities should never be presented in back-to-back.

3. Next, uppercase letters are introduced. Uppercase letters are introduced before lowercase letters because they are easier to discriminate visually than lowercase letters. When letter formations are first presented to a student, their visual system analyzes the vertical, horizontal, and curved orientations of the letters. Therefore, teachers should use think-alouds when instructing how to write the shape of each letter. During think-alouds, teachers verbalize their own thought processes that occur when writing each part of a given letter. Students should be encouraged to do likewise when practicing printing the letters.

4. Once uppercase letters are mastered, lowercase letters can be introduced. High-frequency lowercase letters (*a, e, t*) are introduced prior to low-frequency lowercase letters (*q, x, z*).

5. Once the recognition of letters is mastered, students need ample time manipulating and utilizing the letters. This can be done through sorting, matching, comparing, and writing activities.

Basic Phonetic Principles

The **alphabetic principle** is the understanding of the names and sounds produced by letters, letter patterns, and symbols printed on a page. Through the alphabetic principle, students learn letter-sound correspondence, phonemic awareness, and the application of simple decoding skills such as the sounding out and blending of letter sounds. Since reading is essentially the blending together of multiple letter sounds, the alphabetic principle is crucial in reading development.

As with the instruction of letter recognition, research has revealed the following sequence to be effective in the teaching of the alphabetic principle:

1. Letter-sound relationships need to be taught explicitly and in isolation. The rate at which new letter-sound correspondences can be presented will be unique to the student group. The order in which letters are presented should permit students to read words quickly. Therefore, letter-sound pairs that are used frequently should be presented before letter-sound pairs with lower utility. Similarly, it is suggested to first present consonant letter-sound pairs that can be pronounced in

isolation without distortion (*f, m, s, r*). Instruction of letters that sound similar should not be presented in proximity.

2. Once single-letter and sound combinations are mastered, consonant blends and clusters (*br, cr, gr*) can be presented.

Invented Spellings and Phonetic Principles

When children begin to learn the various letter-sound correspondences, their phonemic awareness begins to overlap with their awareness of orthography and reading. One of the widely accepted strategies to employ when introducing children to letter-sound correspondences is to begin with those correspondences that occur the most frequently in simple English words. In an effort to help build confidence in young learners, educators are encouraged to introduce only a few letter-sound combinations at a time and provide ample opportunities for practice and review before introducing new combinations. Although there is no formally established order for the introduction of letter-sound correspondences, educators are encouraged to consider the following general guidelines, but they should also keep in mind the needs, experiences, and current literacy levels of the students. The following is intended as a general guide only:

1. a	6. n	11. g	16. l	21. x
2. m	7. c	12. h	17. e	22. v
3. t	8. d	13. i	18. r	23. y
4. p	9. u	14. f	19. w	24. z
5. o	10. s	15. b	20. k	25. j
				26. q

As a generally accepted rule, short vowels should be introduced ahead of long vowels, and uppercase letters should be mastered before the introduction of their lowercase counterparts.

Spelling conventions in the English language are primarily concerned with three areas: mechanics, usage, and sentence formation.

Mechanics

For primary students who are just beginning to master the alphabetic principle, educators should first concentrate on proper letter formation, the spelling of high-frequency words and sight words, and offering classroom discussions to promote the sharing of ideas. When children begin to write in sentences to share their thoughts and feelings in print, educators may consider the introduction of an author's chair, in which students read their writing out loud to their classmates.

Although the phonetic spelling or invented spelling that primary students employ in these early stages may not be the conventional spelling of certain words, it allows primary students to practice the art and flow of writing. It works to build their confidence in the writing process. This is not the time for

Phonological Awareness

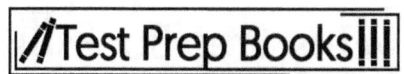

educators to correct spelling, punctuation, or capitalization errors, as young learners may quickly lose interest in writing and may lose self-confidence.

One strategy to employ early on to help students with proper spelling is to ensure there is an easily accessible and updated word wall that employs high-frequency words and sight words. Students should be encouraged to refer to the word wall while they write.

Usage

Usage concerns itself with word order, verb tense, and subject-verb agreement among other areas. As primary children often have a basic knowledge of how to use oral language effectively in order to communicate, this area of spelling conventions may require less initial attention than the mechanics of spelling. During read-aloud and shared reading activities, educators may wish to point out punctuation marks found in print, model how to read these punctuation marks, and periodically discuss their importance in the reading and writing process.

When children begin to engage in writing exercises, educators may wish to prompt self-editing skills by asking if each sentence begins with a capital and ends with a period, question mark, or exclamation point.

Sentence Formation

Verbs, nouns, adverbs, and adjectives all play significant roles in the writing process. However, for primary students, these concepts are fairly complex to understand. One instruction approach that may prove effective is to categorize a number of simple verbs, nouns, adverbs, and adjectives on index cards by color coordination. Educators can then ask one child to choose a noun card and another student to choose a verb card. The children can then face the class and read their words starting with the noun and then the verb. The students can even try reading the verb first followed by the noun. A class discussion can follow, analyzing whether or not the sentences made sense and what words might need to be added to give the sentence more meaning.

Developing Phonemic Awareness for All Learners

Types of Phonemic Awareness Skills

Instruction of phonological awareness includes detecting and identifying word boundaries, syllables, onset/rime, and rhyming words. Each of these skills is explained below.

- **Word boundaries:** Students must be able to identify how many letters are in a word and that spaces between words indicate where a word begins and ends.

- **Syllables:** A syllable is a unit of speech that contains a vowel sound. A syllable does not necessarily have to be surrounded by consonants. Therefore, every syllable has a rime. However, not every syllable has an onset.

- **Onset:** An onset is the beginning sound of any word. For example, /c/ is the onset in the word cat.

- **Rime:** The rime of a word is the sound that follows the word's onset. The /at/ is the rime in the word cat.

- **Syllabification:** Syllabification is the dividing of words into their component syllables. Syllabification should begin with single-syllable words and progress toward multi-syllable words.

- **Rhyming words:** Rhyming words are often almost identical except for their beginning letter(s). Therefore, rhyming is an effective strategy to implement during the analytic phase of phonics development.

Instruction of phonemic awareness includes recognizing, blending, segmenting, deleting, and substituting phonemes. These skills are explained below.

Phoneme Recognition
Phoneme recognition occurs when students recognize that words are made of separate sounds and they are able to distinguish the initial, middle, and final phonemes within words. Initial awareness of phonemes should be done in isolation and not within words. Then, phoneme awareness can be achieved through shared readings that are supplemented with identification activities, such as the identification of rhyming words.

Blending
Sound blending is the ability to mix together two or more sounds or phonemes. For example, a **consonant blend** is a combination of two or more consonants into a single sound such as /cr/ or /sp/. Blending often begins when the teacher models the slow pronunciation of sound parts within a word. Students are to do likewise, with scaffolding provided by the teacher. Eventually, the pronunciation rate is increased, so that the full word is spoken as it would be in normal conversation.

Segmenting
Sound segmentation is the ability to identify the component phonemes in a word. Segmentation begins with simple, single-syllable words. For instance, a teacher might pronounce the word tub and see if students can identify the /t/, /u/, and /b/ sounds. The student must identify all three sounds in order for sound segmentation to be complete.

Deleting
Sound deletion is an oral activity in which one of the phonemes of a spoken word is removed. For example, a teacher may say a word aloud and then ask students to say the word without a specific sound (e.g., "What word would be formed if cat is said without the /c/ sound?"). With repetition, deletion activities can improve phoneme recognition.

Substituting
Like deletion, **substitution** takes place orally and is initiated through modeling. However, instead of deleting a phoneme or syllable, spoken words are manipulated via the substitution of phonemes for others (e.g., "What word would be formed if we change the /b/ in bun to /r/?").

Phonics Knowledge and Decoding Skills

Basic Phonic Elements

Phonics incorporates the alphabetic principle and decoding strategies. Phonics knowledge includes recognizing letter-sound correspondence. Students use phonics to sound out letter sequences and blend the sounds of the letter sequences together in order to form words.

Phonics instruction should begin with the decoding of simple syllable patterns, such as *am* and *map*. Upon mastery of simple patterns, more complex patterns can be introduced, such as *tape* or *spot*. The following characteristics are present in an effective phonics program:

- The goal and purpose are clarified at the beginning of each lesson.
- Visual and concrete material, such as letter cards and dry-erase boards, are used.
- Direct instruction of letter sounds is provided through a series of mini lessons.
- Direct instruction in the decoding of letter sounds found in words is provided, such as sounding out letters and blending sounds into words.
- Students partake in guided and independent practice during which immediate feedback is provided. Activities such as word reading and word sorts, which incorporate previously taught spelling patterns, can reinforce explicit phonics instruction.
- Effective phonics programs allow students to apply new phonics skills in a broad range of reading and writing contexts.

Proper Sequencing of Complex Linguistic Units

Research has shown that phonics and sight-word instruction is best accomplished using the following steps:

1. Phonics instruction should begin with **consonant sounds**. Consonant sounds block the flow of air through the mouth. Consonants can form either continuous or stop sounds. **Continuous sounds** are those that can be said for a long period of time, such as /mmm/. **Stop sounds** are said in short bursts, such as /t/.

2. The following common and regular letter combinations can be taught:

- **Consonant digraphs**: Consonant digraphs are combinations of two or three consonants that work together to make a single sound. Examples of consonant digraphs are sh, ch, and th.
- **Consonant blends**: Consonant blends are sometimes referred to as **consonant clusters**. Consonant blends occur when two or three consonant sounds are blended together to make a single consonant sound. Unlike consonant digraphs, each letter in a consonant blend is identifiable. Examples of consonant blends are gl, gr, pl, sm, and sp.
- **Vowel digraphs**: Vowel digraphs are sets of two vowels that spell a single sound. A diagraph is not a sound. Examples of vowel digraph pairs are ow, ie, ae, ou, ei, ie, and oo.
- **Diphthongs**: Diphthongs are the sounds created by letter/vowel combinations.
- **R- and l- controlled vowels**: These are words in which a vowel sound is controlled in a word that contains an r, l, or ll at its beginning or end. Examples include car, girl, old, or call.

3. Common inflected morphological units can be taught. **Morphological units** include word parts such as affixes or root words. Examples of morphological units that could be presented at this time are suffixes such as *-ed, -er, -est, -ing,* and *-s*.

4. Common word patterns of increasing difficulty are presented. **Word patterns** are made of sequences (or patterns) of vowels (V) and consonants (C). Examples include VC (*ear, egg, eat*, etc.), CVC (*cat, bat, map*, etc.), CCVC (*stop, frog, spot*, etc.), CVVC (*head, lead, dead*, etc.), CVCe (*same, make, rale*, etc.), etc.

5. In this stage, students are taught identification of vowel-consonant patterns and multisyllabic-word syllabication.

6. After syllabication of multisyllabic words, a discussion of why some words are irregular should occur. **Irregular words** are words that are not decodable. Students may struggle decoding some words because the sounds of the letters found within the words do not follow predictable phonics patterns.

7. Time should be allotted for the instruction of common irregular sight words that are not readily decodable. However, this is usually not done until students are able to decode words that follow predictable phonic patterns at a rate of one letter-sound per second. Irregular sight words need to be gradually introduced. Words that are visually similar should not be shown in proximity to one another. The irregular words need to be practiced until students can read them with automaticity. New words are not introduced until the previous sets are mastered. The words are continuously reintroduced and reviewed thereafter.

8. When students first begin reading, they may be able to decode some words that have not yet been introduced to them merely by using letter-sound correspondences. The instruction of irregular words should be applied to these words as well.

Blending Consonant and Vowel Sounds to Decode Single-Syllable Words

The ability to break apart a word into its individual phonemes is referred to as **segmenting**. Segmenting words can greatly aid in a child's ability to recognize, read, and spell an entire word. In literacy instruction, **blending** is when the reader connects segmented parts to create an entire word. Segmenting and blending practice work together like pieces of a puzzle to help children practice newly-acquired vocabulary. Educators can approach segmenting and blending using a multi-sensory approach. For example, a child can manipulate letter blocks to build words and pull them apart. An educator may even ask the child to listen to the word being said and ask him or her to find the letter blocks that build each phoneme, one at a time:

/m/ /u/ /g/

/b/ /a/ /t/

/r/ /u/ /n/

Once children are able to blend and segment phonemes, they are ready for the more complex skill of blending and segmenting syllables, onsets, and rimes. Using the same multi-sensory approach, children may practice blending the syllables of familiar words on a word wall, using letter blocks, paper and pencil, or sounding them out loud. Once they blend the words together, students can then practice segmenting those same words, studying their individual syllables and the letters and sounds that create the words. Educators may again read a word out loud and ask children to write or build the first syllable, followed by the next, and so on. The very same practice can be used to identify the onset. Children can work on writing and/or building this sound followed by the word's rime. Word families and rhyming words are ideal for this type of exercise so that children can more readily see the parts of each word. Using words that rhyme can turn this exercise into a fun and engaging activity.

Phonological Awareness

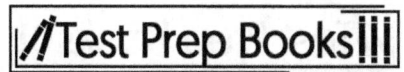

Once children have demonstrated the ability to independently blend and segment phonemes, syllables, onsets, and rimes, educators may present a more challenging exercise that involves substitutions and deletions. As these are more complex skills, children will likely benefit from repeated practice and modeling. Using word families and words that rhyme when teaching this skill will make the activity more enjoyable, and it will also greatly aid in a child's overall comprehension.

Substitution and Deletion Using Onset and Rime				
Word	Onset Deletion	Rime Deletion	Onset Substitution	Rime Substitution
Run	un	r	Fun	rat
Bun	un	b	Gun	bat
Sun	un	s	Nun	sat

Substitution and Deletion Using Phonemes		
Word	Phoneme Substitution	Phoneme Deletion
Sit	sat	si
Bit	bat	bi
Hit	hat	hi

Substitution and Deletion Using Syllables		
Word	Syllable Substitution	Syllable Deletion
cement	lament or, cedar	ce
moment	statement, or motive	mo
basement	movement, or baseball	base

Consonant-Vowel Patterns

While reading has much to do with conceptual knowledge of English and awareness of the structures and rules of the language, recognizing word patterns can also help students see basic English principles. Being able to recognize familiar word patterns essentially helps students decode the pronunciation and even the meaning of unfamiliar words by recognizing core linguistic components.

The first step in identifying patterns is knowing how to sort words. When describing and searching for word patterns, sound is key. To begin, instructors can have students (or themselves) list single-syllable words that share similar beginnings, endings, and vowel sounds. Examining **affixes** (the letters before or after the root word), which change a word's initial meaning, is also key. For example, students can recognize that the *a* used in *bat* and *cat* sound the same. Recognizing this sorting method provides insight on how to pronounce the words *that* or *fat*. Thus, students gain a tool for decoding words they haven't seen before.

Teachers should also examine words that are spelled differently but sound the same. For example, *veer*, *near*, and *tier* share a sound pattern but are spelled differently. This sheds light on how the vowels *ee*, *ea*, and *ie* sound between consonants. For an activity, students can group vowel combinations into columns that indicate a shared sound to help them recognize the connection between sound and spelling patterns. Another engaging activity would be to have students create small poems that use words with a specific sound. For example, using the vowel *i*, students can be encouraged to create a rhyme with three words, each with one syllable. The results should share common vowel and consonant sounds, such as *tip*, *ship*, and *dip* or *fig*, *lip*, and *skid*. Note how the vowel remains constant even while the consonants change.

Some single-syllable words, such as common sight words, have no clear pattern. The best way to teach these words (*the*, *to*, and others) is to have students visualize and learn them just as they are. One easy activity would be to play bingo or a similar visual game using single-syllable sight words to build familiarity with the everyday terms.

Decoding Multisyllabic Words

The methodology of grouping and recognizing patterns in single-syllable words can also apply to multisyllable words. However, because these words are more complex, the pattern scope must be broader. Again, teachers must reexamine similar-sounding vowel groups and consonant relationships as with singular-syllable words. It may also help to review the six patterns of syllable spelling format: open, closed, vowel team, silent vowel *e*, consonant *le*, and *r*-controlled patterns.

As a class activity, students can spend time grouping individual words into the spelling formats to demonstrate their knowledge of English sounds and how the letters function in the words. Once explaining the categories, the instructor can even name a word and have the students say it back and then group the word into an appropriate category. For example, the word *throat* has a kind of *oh* sound because of the vowel team *oa*. Instructors should also distinguish closed- and open-syllable spelling patterns. **Open** reflects a long vowel ending sound, such as *tiger,* with an exaggerated *-er* sounding ending; alternately, the **closed** pattern reflects a short vowel sound toward the end as seen in the word *darken*.

The **r-controlled vowels** are also important to highlight. Words such as *fur* and *car* stand out because of how the *r* sounds more prevalent than the vowel. To practice this, students can list words such as *cart*, *short, turtle,* and *fertile* on the board so they can have a visual reference, or the teacher can go around the class and have students name such words aloud. Again, it's important to hear the words and examine them visually in order for students to grasp how the words function and operate.

With multisyllable words, it's important to review consonant diagraphs and how they function. Because there are many diagraphs with different pronunciations, it's important to demonstrate how they differ in various words, such as the *ch* in *Christmas* and *charity*. Students should also be able to compare how moving diagraphs within words alter pronunciations, such as with *anchor* or *pitch,* respectively.

When it comes to approaching multisyllable words in general, teachers should emphasize sounding out the words in order to grasp the pronunciation. Another good strategy for learning larger words is to have students break a word down by syllables and then combine them to complete the whole word. Again, an interactive approach to these principles will help students grasp the material more easily.

Word-Analysis Skills for Decoding and Encoding Words

Phonemic Awareness in Reading Development

A **phoneme** is the smallest unit of sound in a given language and is one aspect under the umbrella of skills associated with phonological awareness. A child demonstrates phonemic awareness when identifying rhymes, recognizing alliterations, and isolating specific sounds inside a word or a set of words. Students who demonstrate basic phonemic awareness will eventually also be able to independently and appropriately blend together a variety of phonemes.

Some classroom strategies to strengthen phonemic awareness may include:

- Introduction to nursery rhymes and word play
- Speech discrimination techniques to train the ear to hear more accurately
- Repeated instruction connecting sounds to letters and blending sounds
- Use of visual images coupled with corresponding sounds and words
- Teaching speech sounds through direct instruction
- Comparing known to unfamiliar words
- Practicing pronunciation of newly introduced letters, letter combinations, and words
- Practicing word decoding
- Differentiating similar sounding words

Development of Phonemic-Awareness Skills

Age-appropriate and developmentally appropriate instruction for phonological and phonemic awareness is key to helping children strengthen their reading and writing skills. Phonological and phonemic awareness, or PPA, instruction works to enhance correct speech, improve understanding and application of accurate letter-to-sound correspondence, and strengthen spelling skills. Since skill-building involving phonemes is not a natural process but needs to be taught, PPA instruction is especially important for children who have limited access and exposure to reading materials and who lack familial encouragement to read. Strategies that educators can implement include leading word and sound games, focusing on phoneme skill-building activities, and ensuring all activities focus on the fun, playful nature of words and sounds instead of rote memorization and drilling techniques.

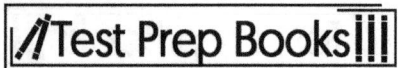

Phonological Awareness

Interaction of Phonics, Syntax, and Semantics

Vocabulary

Vocabulary consists of the bank of words that children can understand and apply fluently in order to communicate effectively. A strong vocabulary and word recognition base enables children to access prior knowledge and experiences in order to make connections in written texts. A strong vocabulary also allows children to express ideas, learn new concepts, and decode the meanings of unfamiliar words by using context clues. Conversely, if a child's vocabulary knowledge is limited and does not steadily increase, reading comprehension will be negatively affected. If children become frustrated with their lack of understanding of written texts, they will likely choose to only read texts at their comfort level or refuse to read altogether. With direct instruction, educators introduce specific words to pre-teach before reading, or examine word roots, prefixes, and suffixes. Through indirect instruction, educators ensure that students are regularly exposed to new words. This engages students in high-quality conversations and social interactions and provides access to a wide variety of challenging and enjoyable reading material.

Morphology

Morphology is the study of the structure and the formation of words. A **phoneme** is the smallest unit of sound that does not necessarily carry meaning. Essentially, phonemes are combined to form words, and words are combined to form sentences. Morphology looks at the smallest meaningful part of a word, known as a **morpheme**. In contrast to a phoneme, a morpheme must carry a sound and a meaning. Free morphemes are those that can stand alone, carrying both sound and meaning, as in the following words: *girl, boy, man,* and *lady*. Just as the name suggests, **bound morphemes** are bound to other morphemes in order to carry meaning. Examples of bound morphemes include: *ish, ness, ly,* and *dis*.

Semantics

Semantics is the branch of linguistics that studies the meanings of words. Morphemes, words, phrases, and sentences all carry distinct meanings. The way these individual parts are arranged can have a significant effect on meaning. In order to construct language, children must be able to use semantics to arrange and rearrange words to achieve the particular meaning they are striving for. Activities that teach semantics revolve around teaching the arrangement of word parts (morphology) and root words, and then the teaching of vocabulary. Moving from vocabulary words into studying sentences and sentence structure leads children to learn how to use context clues to determine meaning and to understand anomalies such as metaphors, idioms, and allusions.

There are five types of semantic relationships that are critical to understand:

Hyponyms refer to a relationship between words where general words have multiple more-specific words (hyponyms) that fall into the same category (e.g., horse: mare, stallion, foal, Appaloosa, Clydesdale).

Meronyms refer to a relationship between words where a whole word has multiple parts (meronyms) that comprise it (e.g., horse: tail, mane, hooves, ears).

Synonyms refer to words that have the same meaning as another word (e.g., instructor/teacher/educator, canine/dog, feline/cat, herbivore/vegetarian).

Antonyms refer to words that have the opposite meaning as another word (e.g., true/false, up/down, in/out, right/wrong).

Homonyms refer to words that are spelled the same (**homographs**) or sound the same (**homophones**) but mean different things (e.g., there/their/they're, two/too/to, principal/principle, plain/plane, (kitchen) sink/ sink (down as in water)).

Syntax

With its origins from the Greek word, "syntaxis," which means arrangement, **syntax** is the study of phrase and sentence formation. The study of syntax focuses on the ways in which specific words can be combined to create coherent meaning. For example: the simple rearrangement of the words, "I can run," is different from the question, "Can I run?" which is also different from the meaningless "Run I can."

The following methods can be used to teach syntax:

- Proper Syntax Modeling: Students don't need to be corrected for improper syntax. Instead, they should be shown ways to rephrase what they said with proper syntax. If a student says, "Run I can," then the teacher should say, "Oh, you can run how fast?" This puts syntax in place with conversational skills.

- Open-Ended Sentences: Students can complete open-ended sentences with proper syntax both orally and in written format, or they can correct sentences that have improper syntax so that they make sense.

- Listening for Syntax: Syntax is auditory. Students can often hear a syntax error before they can see it in writing. Teachers should have students use word cards or word magnets to arrange and rearrange simple sentences and read them aloud to check for syntax.

- Repetition: Syntax can be practiced by using songs, poems, and rhymes for repetitive automation.

Pragmatics

Pragmatics is the study of what words mean in certain situations. It helps to understand the intentions and interpretations of intentions through words used in human interaction. Different listeners and different situations call for different language and intonations of language. When people engage in a conversation, it is usually to convey a certain message, and the message (even using the same words) can change depending on the setting and the audience. The more fluent the speaker, the more success she or he will have in conveying the intended message.

The following methods can be used to teach pragmatics:

- When students state something incorrectly, a response can be given to what they intended to say in the first place. For instance, if a student says, "That's how it didn't happen." Then the teacher might say, "Of course, that's not how it happened." Instead of putting students on defense by being corrected, this method puts them at ease and helps them learn.

- Role-playing conversations with different people in different situations can help teach pragmatics. For example, pretend playing can be used where a situation remains the same but the audience changes, or the audience stays the same but the situations change. This can be followed with a discussion about how language and intonations change too.

- Different ways to convey a message can be used, such as asking vs. persuading, or giving direct vs. indirect requests and polite vs. impolite messages.

- Various non-verbal signals can be used to see how they change pragmatics. For example, students can be encouraged to use mismatched words and facial expressions, such as angry words while smiling or happy words while pretending to cry.

Developing Word Consciousness and Vocabulary Knowledge

Word consciousness can be developed through structural analysis of word parts and words origins. Identification of word segments will enable students to more readily master new words.

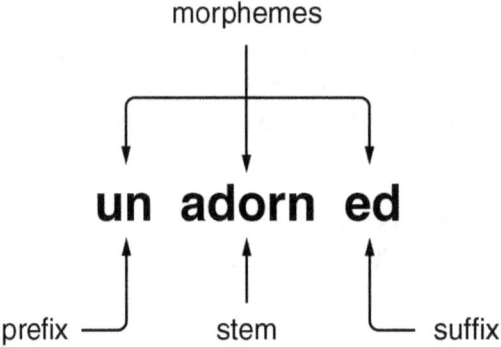

Students can develop a love of words through word games, which create a safe environment to take linguistic risks and feel successful. Examples include sight word games, word memory games, or games that require students to create new words using an assigned list of affixes and roots.

A **word sort** is an example of a word game that can be used to develop word consciousness. Using a set of word cards prepared by the teacher, students decide how to separate the cards into categories. Students are then asked to explain why they grouped a set of words together.

Students also learn to love words by sharing new and interesting words they encounter through independent reading or when they are taught new words explicitly by the teacher. Students can share new words on an online word blog or word cloud, a word wall within the classroom, or a word list contained within a notebook. These tools help to personalize vocabulary instruction while improving students' flexibility and fluency.

Schema development for easier word acquisition can be developed by dividing these word lists into categories based on similarities or differences. The list of new words should be referred to often in order to increase the students' exposure. To further strengthen comprehension, students should be required to utilize the words in writing and discussion activities.

Word Reference Materials

Words can have different meanings depending on how they are used in a text. There are several methods for helping students decipher word meanings:

Students should be taught to effectively use a dictionary and a thesaurus, including digital dictionaries and resources. Students need to know how to read the dictionary, so they understand that there can be more than one meaning for a particular word. Dictionaries also help teach word pronunciation and syllables. A thesaurus teaches antonyms and synonyms. Once students know the correct meaning and pronunciation, they are able to better understand the context of the word in the text.

High-Frequency, Sight, and Irregularly Spelled Words

Automatic Word Recognition

Word recognition occurs when students are able to correctly and automatically recognize and read a word. Phonics and sight word instruction help with the promotion of accurate and automatic word identification and word recognition. Once students are able to readily identify and recognize words, their attention is not devoted toward the dissection of word interpretation, and they can focus on the meaning of the text, supporting reading comprehension skills.

Phonics instruction stresses letter-sound correspondences and the manipulation of phonemes. Through phonics instruction, students discover the different sounds of a spoken language and how a written language's letters and symbols relate to one another. It is through the application of phonics principles that students are able to decode words. When a word is **decoded**, the letters that make up the printed word are translated into sounds. When students are able to recognize and manipulate letter-sound relationships of single-syllable words, they are able to apply such relationships to decode more complex words. In this way, phonics aids reading fluency and reading comprehension.

Sight words, sometimes referred to as **high-frequency words**, are words that are used often but may not follow the regular principles of phonics. Sight words may also be defined as words that students are able to readily recognize and read without having to sound them out. Students are encouraged to memorize words by sight so their reading fluency is not deterred through the frequent decoding of regularly-occurring irregular words. In this way, sight word recognition aids reading fluency and reading comprehension.

Applying Word Analysis Skills

Phonics and decoding skills aid the analysis of new words. **Word analysis** is the ability to recognize the relationships between the spelling, syllabication, and pronunciation of new and/or unfamiliar words. Having a clear understanding of word structure, orthography, and the meaning of morphemes also aid in the analysis of new words.

However, not all words follow predictable phonics patterns, morphology, or orthography. Such irregular words must be committed to memory and are called sight words.

Phonics skills, syllabic skills, structural analysis, word analysis, and memorization of sight words lead to word recognition automaticity. **Word recognition** is the ability to correctly and automatically recognize words in or out of context. Word recognition is a prerequisite for fluent reading and reading comprehension.

Practice Quiz

1. Words a child encounters and sees in everyday life are an example of which of the following?
    a. One-to-one correspondence
    b. Environmental print
    c. Directionality of print
    d. Sight words

2. A teacher who uses a word wall is actively encouraging which of the following?
    a. Sight words
    b. Phonetic spelling
    c. Vocabulary
    d. Sentence building

3. Although there is no formally established method for teaching letters and sounds, which of the following is the recommended starting point for a teacher?
    a. Alphabetical order because it is familiar
    b. The letters in a student's name
    c. The letters that appear most often in English
    d. Letters and sounds from words the students know well

4. When teaching letters, teachers should do which of the following?
    a. Teach uppercase and lowercase letters at the same time.
    b. Teach letters with similar shapes or sounds at the same time.
    c. Introduce low-frequency letters first.
    d. Talk students through the process and thoughts when drawing a letter.

5. Read-alouds are valuable because they teach students which of the following?
    a. Sight words
    b. One-to-one correspondence
    c. Phonics
    d. Letter shapes

See answers on the next page.

Answer Explanations

1. B: Environmental print includes the words a child is exposed to in daily life, such as street signs or cereal boxes. Choice *A*, one-to-one correspondence, refers to matching written words to spoken words and is therefore incorrect. Choice *C* is incorrect because print directionality refers to a student's understanding of reading print from left to write (for the word, the sentence, and in a book). Finally, sight words, Choice *D,* are the words a young reader has learned "on sight" without having to break them down or decode them.

2. A: Word walls are incredibly useful in helping students learn those words on sight, which facilitates their reading skills, particularly their speed and flow. Phonetic spelling, Choice *B*, is the invented spelling of early language learners as they spell words the way they sound. This is not shown on word walls and is therefore incorrect. Choice *C* is incorrect; learning vocabulary is not the goal of a word wall. A word wall is building on existing knowledge, or already-known words. Choice *D* is incorrect. Although sentence building is starting to happen at this time, as students learn more words, word walls are a reading strategy, not a writing strategy.

3. C: A teacher should start with letters and letter combinations and sounds that appear most frequently in simple English words and then slowly introduce more. Choice *A* is incorrect. Although students are familiar with the alphabet, this order is not demonstrative of the sounds they will come into contact with most frequently, and there are sounds and letters that are very similar in proximity that may be confusing for young learners (for example, *b* and *d, v* and *w*). Choice *B* is incorrect. Although this is a great strategy for teaching the writing of letters, there are likely too many names in a classroom, and some of them are probably very different or complicated, so this strategy may result in confusing combinations. Much like the alphabet, teachers may end up with combinations that are difficult for early learners to differentiate. Choice *D* is also incorrect. Students may know quite a few words; however, they may be different from one another, and again, may include combinations that are too difficult for students to build confidence early on.

4. D: As a teacher is demonstrating how to draw a letter, they should walk and talk a student through the thought process of think-aloud. This method enables teachers to demonstrate the vertical, curved, and horizontal shapes that form letters. Choice *A* is incorrect because uppercase letters are easier to distinguish and should therefore be taught first. Once students are familiar with them, teachers should move on to lowercase letters. Choice *B* is incorrect because students may easily confuse these letters, such as *b* and *p,* which both use a loop and a vertical line. Choice *C* is incorrect because the letters students will see most often and may recognize first should be among the first they learn.

5. B: Read-alouds, in which a teacher can show the students the words as they are being read, allow students to begin to connect a spoken word to a written word, also knowns as *one-to-one correspondence.* Choice *A* is incorrect because sight words are taught through strategies such as word walls, not read-aloud activities. They are words students can identify on sight. Choice *C* is incorrect because phonics are taught through understanding individual letters as well as letter blends. Finally, read-alouds do not allow the kind of detailed and methodical analysis of shapes and lines to facilitate the teaching of letter shapes, so Choice *D* is incorrect.

Vocabulary Acquisition

Vocabulary Acquisition and Use

Acquiring and Using Vocabulary

There are three tiers of vocabulary:

Tier 1 is composed of basic vocabulary words that appear often in everyday speech (for example, "cat," "run," "almost"). Teachers do not usually need to teach these words, as children know them before entering grade school. Because they are so familiar, they make excellent words for new readers.

Tier 2 features words that occur fairly often in English but are more complicated than Tier 1 words or have multiple meanings. For example, "profitable," "eager," and "execute" are all Tier 2 words. This is the level of vocabulary in which students progress furthest during their education, and it is often used to measure student progress.

Tier 3 includes words that appear only in specialized contexts. Students typically learn these words in context; for example, students learn "heterozygous" in biology class and "Industrial Revolution" in history.

There are also two types of vocabulary knowledge:

- **Recognition** refers to a student's ability to understand a word. For example, a student who understands the word "heinous" when it appears but would be unable to think of the word without reading or hearing it demonstrates recognition.

- **Production** is the capacity to use the word properly without reading or hearing it. A student who can use the word "aptitude" correctly without being prompted is said to be *producing* the word. Production necessitates a deeper level of vocabulary knowledge than recognition, as the student must remember the word well enough to think of it by themselves.

Using Context

Reference materials are the most obvious way students can independently learn the definition and pronunciation of new vocabulary terms.

When using **contextual strategies**, students are introduced to new words indirectly within a sentence or paragraph. Contextual strategies require students to infer the meaning of a word by utilizing semantic and contextual clues.

The use of appositives and parenthetical elements can be very effective contextual strategies. **Appositives** are words or a group of words that add meaning or define a term that directly precedes them. An example of a sentence that includes apposition is: "Strawberries, heart-shaped and red berries, are delicious when eaten right off of the vine." In this sentence, the definition of strawberries ("heart shaped and red berries") directly follows the term and is introduced with and closes with a comma. **Parenthetical elements** are specific types of appositives that add details to a term but not necessarily a definition. For example: "My cat, the sweetest in the whole world, didn't come home last

Vocabulary Acquisition

night." In this sentence, the parenthetical element ("the sweetest in the whole world") further describes the cat but does not provide a definition of the word "cat."

Structural analysis skills are beneficial in the pronunciation of new words. When readers use **structural analysis**, they recognize affixes or roots as meaningful word parts within a word. When a new word doesn't contain parts that are recognized by a student, the reader can use phonic letter–sound patterns to divide the word into syllables. The word parts can then be combined to yield the proper pronunciation.

Word maps are visual organizers that promote structural analysis skills for vocabulary development. **Word maps** may require students to define or provide synonyms, antonyms, and pictures for given vocabulary terms. Alternatively, **morphological maps** may be used to relate words that share a common morpheme.

Similarly, **word webs** are used to compare and classify a list of words. Word webs show relationships between new words and a student's background knowledge. With the main concept placed centrally within the word web, secondary and tertiary terms stem off from this central concept.

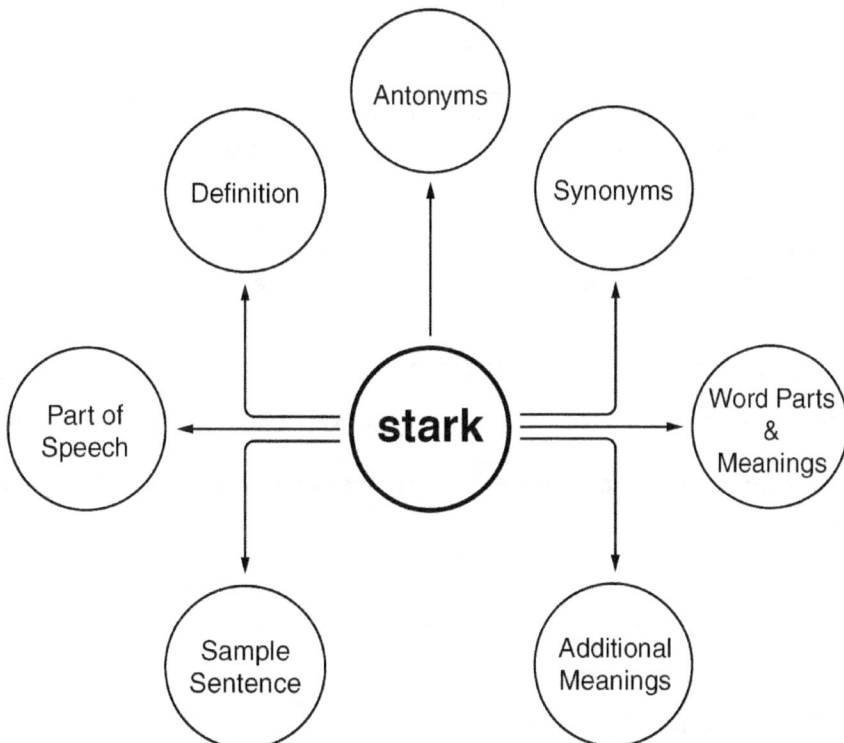

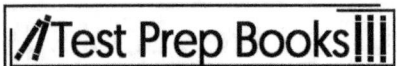

Vocabulary Acquisition

The table below identifies additional ways in which teachers can help students independently define unfamiliar words or words with multiple meanings:

Strategy	Examples
By Definition: Look up the word in a dictionary or thesaurus. Helps students realize that a single word can have multiple meanings.	Her favorite fruit to eat was a date. He went on a date with his girlfriend.
By Example: Invite students to offer their own examples, or to state their understanding following your own examples.	A myth is a story attempting to explain a natural phenomenon, such as the story of Prometheus to understand fire.
By Synonym: Understand that words have many different meanings. Some words are better synonyms than others.	She was very happy that day; her face was *radiant* with joy.
By Antonym: Teach student to look for words that have opposite meanings if the context of the sentence calls for its opposite.	Hannah was not happy that day; she was, in fact, very *depressed*.
By Apposition: Apposition is when the definition is given within the sentence.	The mango, a round, yellow, juicy fruit with an enormous seed in the middle, was ripe enough to eat.
By Origin: Identify Greek and Latin roots to figure out meanings of words.	In the word *hypertension*, the root "*hyper*" is a Greek word meaning "above" or "over."
By Context: Identifying what a word means by the surrounding text.	Water evaporates when it becomes hot, and the liquid turns into gas.

Vocabulary Acquisition and Use in Speaking and Listening, Reading and Writing

Vocabulary Acquisition

Vocabulary used throughout informational texts is generally quite different than vocabulary found in fictional print. For this reason, it is imperative that educators help children strengthen and increase their vocabulary inventory so that they can eventually become successful at reading and understanding informational text.

Vocabulary Acquisition

For instance, educators can point out *signal words* throughout texts to help children more readily and accurately identify the author's purpose. There are specific vocabulary words that authors employ that spotlight the author's intent. For instance, if authors wish to list examples to support a main idea, they may use vocabulary such as *for example*, *such as*, or *as illustrated*. When displaying the chronological order of events, authors may use *first*, *lastly*, *before*, and *finally*. Some common compare and contrast vocabulary words include *but*, *same as*, *similar to*, *as opposed to*, and *however*. There are several key phrases that signal cause and effect relationships, including *because of*, *as a result of*, and *in order to*.

Using word walls and personal dictionaries, sorting vocabulary words according to theme, introducing text maps, and teaching children to become familiar with sidebars and glossaries in informational texts, educators will help expand their students' vocabulary and strengthen their ability to read and comprehend informational texts successfully.

One of the most valuable strategies for helping children to read and understand new words is **pre-teaching**. In this strategy, educators select what they evaluate to be the unfamiliar words in the text and then introduce them to the class before reading. Educators using this method should be careful not to simply ask the children to read the text and then spell the new words correctly. They should also provide clear definitions and give the children the opportunity to read these words in various sentences to decipher word meaning. This method can dramatically reduce how often children stop reading in order to reflect on unknown words. Educators are often unsure as to whether to correct every mispronounced word a child makes when reading. If the mispronounced word still makes sense, it is sometimes better to allow the child to continue to read, since the more the child stops, the more the child's reading comprehension and fluency are negatively affected.

Vocabulary knowledge is an indicator and predictor of comprehension. If students find a match between a word within a text and a word that they've learned through listening and speaking, they are likelier to recognize and understand the meaning of the word in the written context. As the students will spend less time decoding and interpreting the word, they are likelier to read fluently and with comprehension. In contrast, if students cannot connect a written word to a word within their speaking or listening vocabulary, their fluency and comprehension may be interrupted. This proves to be true even if the student is able to correctly pronounce the word.

Methods for Scaffolding the Learning of Standard American English

English Language Learners (ELLs) or students with varying dialects may need alternate methods of instruction when it comes to the learning of standard American English. Scaffolding refers to techniques used that allow students to progress toward a greater level of understanding on an increasingly independent level. The teacher will help the student by gradually removing aid until the student can perform the task on their own. Although there are many different scaffolding techniques, a few common ones are presented below:

Connecting New Information to Prior Learning
When using the process of scaffolding, it's important that the ELL student be guided through the activities from the start. Teachers will determine what level of aid to give to the student depending on their language level. One important method of scaffolding is using previous experience to connect to new information. Teachers should be knowledgeable of students' culture and world experiences in order to synthesize new and old information. Cultural relevance in the ELL framework is crucial for the student to understand the importance of what's being taught.

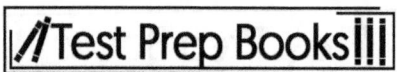

Vocabulary Acquisition

Pre-Teach Academic Vocabulary Outright

Another method of scaffolding is the practice of teaching vocabulary before full immersion is taken place in the English language. Again, a collaborative effort will be most effective for this sort of learning experience. Having students work together to understand the vocabulary word, its meaning, as well as its idiomatic expressions along with frequent visits from the teacher might be a chance to learn vocabulary while also engaging in proximal social interactions. Word walls are also suggested at all levels to help students pronounce unfamiliar words as well as having visual contact with the word along with the auditory experience.

Make Lessons Visual by Using Graphic Organizers

Many students are visual learners, and even if they are not, visual learning is an appropriate aid to many other kinds of learners. This method of scaffolding is also beneficial in helping students develop creativity and work with others to collaboratively assist in each other's creativity and ideas. Graphic organizers include webs, Venn diagrams, story boards, KWL charts, spider maps, and charts, all of which help students organize information and develop higher-level thinking.

Engage English Learners in Discourse

Practicing language "out loud" creates a stimulating environment wherein the student can collaboratively work with others to immerse themselves in social and academic discourse. It's important to make sure academic language is included in this activity, as it is harder to learn and takes a structured environment facilitated by the instructor. Engagement in academic conversations can come before or during social conversations as well. Social conversation may come easier, but academic conversation is important to the classroom as well to aid in development toward future research, writing, and career development.

Independent Word Learning Strategies

Word-Reference Materials

Reference materials are indispensable tools for beginners and experts alike. Becoming a competent English communicator doesn't necessarily mean memorizing every single rule about spelling, grammar, or punctuation; rather, it means knowing where and how to find accurate information about the rules of English usage. Students of English have a wide variety of reference materials available to them, and in an increasingly digitized world, more and more of these materials can be found online or as easily-accessible phone applications. Educators should introduce students to different types of reference materials as well as when and how to use them.

Context

Children who are developing reading fluency and comprehension skills can become frustrated when presented with unfamiliar words in a given text. With direct phonics instruction, educators can teach children to decode words and then use context clues to define the words while reading. If children have a strong enough understanding of language structures, including nouns and verbs, educators can ask them to consider what part of speech the unknown word might be based on and where it might fit into the sentence. Other useful strategies involve **self-monitoring**, in which children are asked to think as they read and ask themselves if what they have just read makes sense. Focusing on visual clues, such as drawings and photographs, may give children valuable insight into deciphering unknown words. Looking for the word in another section of the text to see how it relates to the overall meaning could give a clue

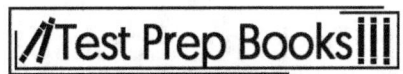

Vocabulary Acquisition

to the new vocabulary word. Spelling the word out loud or looking for word chunks, prefixes, and suffixes, as well as demonstrating how to segment the unknown word into its individual syllables, may also be effective strategies to employ.

Spell Check

Most word processing software programs come equipped with a spell-checking feature. Web browsers and personal devices like smartphones and tablets may also have a spell checker enabled. **Spell check** automatically detects misspelled words and suggests alternate spellings. Many writers have come to rely on spell check due to its convenience and ease of use. However, there are some caveats to using spell check—it only checks whether a word is spelled correctly, not if it is used correctly. As discussed above, there are numerous examples of commonly-confused words in English, the misuse of which may not be detected by a spell checker. Many word processing programs do integrate spell checking and grammar checking functions, however. Thus, although running a spell check is an important part of reviewing any piece of writing, it should not be the only step of the review process. Further, spell checkers recommend correctly-spelled words based on an approximation of the misspelled word, so writers need to be somewhat close to the correct spelling in order for spell check to be useful.

Dictionary

Dictionaries are readily available in print, digital formats, and as mobile apps. A dictionary offers a wealth of information to users. First, in the absence of spell checking software, a dictionary can be used to identify correct spelling and to determine the word's pronunciation—often written using the International Phonetic Alphabet (IPA). Perhaps the best-known feature of a dictionary is its explanation of a word's meanings, as a single word can have multiple definitions. A dictionary organizes these definitions based on their parts of speech and then arranges them from most to least commonly used meanings or from oldest to most modern usage. Many dictionaries also offer information about a word's etymology and usage. With all these functions, then, a dictionary is a basic, essential tool in many situations. Students can turn to a dictionary when they encounter an unfamiliar word or when they see a familiar word used in a new way.

There are many dictionaries to choose from, but perhaps the most highly respected source is the *Oxford English Dictionary* (OED). The OED is a historical dictionary, and as such, all entries include quotes of the word as it has been used throughout history. Users of the OED can get a deeper sense of a word's evolution over time and in different parts of the world. Another standard dictionary in America is *Merriam-Webster*.

Thesaurus

Whereas a dictionary entry lists a word's definitions, a **thesaurus** entry lists a word's synonyms and antonyms—i.e., words with similar and opposite meanings, respectively. A dictionary can be used to find out what a word means and where it came from, and a thesaurus can be used to understand a word's relationship to other words. A thesaurus can be a powerful vocabulary-building tool. By becoming familiar with synonyms and antonyms, students will be more equipped to use a broad range of vocabulary in their speech and writing. Of course, one thing to be aware of when using a thesaurus is that most words do not have exact synonyms. Rather, there are slight nuances of meaning that can make one word more appropriate than another in a given context. In this case, it is often to the user's advantage to consult a thesaurus side-by-side with a dictionary to confirm any differences in usage between two synonyms. Some digital sources, such as *Dictionary.com*, integrate a dictionary and a thesaurus.

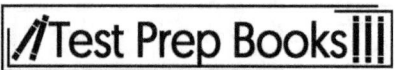

Generally, though, a thesaurus is a useful tool to help writers add variety and precision to their word choice. Consulting a thesaurus can help students elevate their writing to an appropriate academic level by replacing vague or overused words with more expressive or academic ones. Also, word processors often offer a built-in thesaurus, making it easy for writers to look up synonyms and vary word choice as they work.

Glossary

A **glossary** is similar to a dictionary in that it offers an explanation of terms. However, while a dictionary attempts to cover every word in a language, a glossary only focuses on those terms relevant to a specific field. Also, a glossary entry is more likely to offer a longer explanation of a term and its relevance within that field. Glossaries are often found at the back of textbooks or other nonfiction publications in order to explain new or unfamiliar terms to readers. A glossary may also be an entire book on its own that covers all of the essential terms and concepts within a particular profession, field, or other specialized area of knowledge. Thus, for learners seeking general definitions of terms from any context, a dictionary is an appropriate reference source, but for students of specialized fields, a glossary will usually provide more in-depth information.

Style Manual

Many rules of English usage are standard, but other rules may be more subjective. An example can be seen in the following structures:

> I went to the store and bought eggs, milk, and bread.

> I went to the store and bought eggs, milk and bread.

The final comma in a list before *and* or *or* is known as an **Oxford comma**. It is recommended in some styles, but not in others. To determine the appropriate use of the Oxford comma, writers can consult a style manual.

A **style manual** is a comprehensive collection of guidelines for language use and document formatting. Some fields refer to a common style guide—e.g., the Associated Press or *AP Stylebook*, a standard in American journalism. Individual organizations may rely on their own house style. Regardless, the purpose of a style manual is to ensure uniformity across all documents. Style manuals explain things such as how to format titles, when to write out numbers or use numerals, and how to cite sources. Because there are many different style guides, students should know how and when to consult an appropriate guide. *The Chicago Manual of Style* is common in the publication of books and academic journals. The Modern Language Association style (MLA) is another commonly used academic style format, while the American Psychological Association style (APA) may be used for scientific publications. Familiarity with using a style guide is particularly important for students who are college bound or pursuing careers in academic or professional writing.

In the examples above, the Oxford comma is recommended by the Chicago Manual of Style, so sentence A would be correct if the writer is using this style. But the comma is not recommended by the *AP Stylebook*, so sentence B would be correct if the writer is using the AP style.

General Grammar and Style References

Any language arts textbook should offer general grammatical and stylistic advice to students, but there are a few well-respected texts that can also be used for reference. *Elements of Style* by William Strunk is regularly assigned to students as a guide on effective written communication, including how to avoid common usage mistakes and how to make the most of parallel structure. *Garner's Modern American Usage* by Bryan Garner is another text that guides students on how to achieve precision and understandability in their writing. Whereas other reference sources discussed above tend to address specific language concerns, these types of texts offer a more holistic approach to cultivating effective language skills.

Electronic Resources

With print texts, it is easy to identify the authors and their credentials, as well as the publisher and their reputation. With electronic resources like websites, though, it can be trickier to assess the reliability of information. Students should be alert when gathering information from the Internet. Understanding the significance of website **domains**—which include identification strings of a site—can help. Website domains ending in *.edu* are educational sites and tend to offer more reliable research in their field. A *.org* ending tends to be used by nonprofit organizations and other community groups, *.com* indicates a privately-owned website, and a *.gov* site is run by the government. Websites affiliated with official organizations, research groups, or institutes of learning are more likely to offer relevant, fact-checked, and reliable information.

Conversational, Academic, and Domain-Specific Words

Teaching New Words to Diverse Learners

When teaching your students new words, the most important factor is timing. Teaching words before students encounter them in a text helps students avoid confusion while reading. This method is useful for students who struggle with reading comprehension, and it can help make complex texts less overwhelming. For example, you might want to pre-teach words before your students read a book that includes many new scientific words. However, this teaching method can easily become boring. Make sure to engage students by giving examples, using the word in context, and using pictures for younger students.

Teaching students words as they encounter them in the text is useful because it is easier to learn words in context instead of relying on a definition. However, this method will be too disruptive if the text is full of new words. So while a teacher could certainly teach words like "simultaneous" as they appear in a novel, teaching a long list of scientific words as they appear would break up the reading too much and frustrate the students.

Teaching words after students have completed the reading is useful when you are teaching children how to define new words by themselves. For example, the teacher could have students write down words they do not understand and look them up in a dictionary.

Teachers should also teach students word learning strategies so that they can gain vocabulary by themselves. Here are some effective strategies.

- Teaching students how to use dictionaries enables them to learn words independently. You can engage students by having them collect and define new words in a text, or by holding competitions to see who can use the dictionary faster.

- Contextual clues are the elements of a text that surround a word and hint at its meaning. For example, consider the following sentence: "He decided to litigate, so he hired a lawyer." A student could guess that "litigate" means "sue" by recognizing the cause and effect relationship between "decided to litigate" and "hired a lawyer." In this case, "so" is the contextual clue. Another example of a contextual clue is contrast. If a student reads that "dogs are energetic, but cats are lethargic," they can use the word "but" to determine that "lethargic" is the opposite of "energetic."

- **Morphemic analysis** is defining words by breaking them into parts. A morpheme is a word part or unit of meaning; for example, the word "tirelessness" includes the morphemes "tire," "less," and "ness." If students know that "less" means "without" and "ness" turns adjectives into nouns, they can deduce the meaning of "tirelessness."

Practice Quiz

1. Antibody is an example of what kind of vocabulary word?
    a. Tier 1 Basic
    b. Recognized
    c. Tier 2 Complicated
    d. Tier 3 Specialized

2. A teacher who provides a connection between an English language learner's cultural background and new vocabulary is using which strategy?
    a. Scaffolding
    b. Collaboration
    c. Discourse
    d. Relevance

3. A teacher who creates lessons around prefixes is teaching which vocabulary acquisition strategy?
    a. Contextual analysis
    b. Etymological analysis
    c. Morphemic analysis
    d. Inferential analysis

4. Teachers can encourage vocabulary self-learning by introducing reference tools such as a thesaurus. A thesaurus should be paired with which of the following to help students discover nuances between synonyms?
    a. Glossary
    b. Dictionary
    c. Style manual
    d. Spell-check

See answers on the next page.

Answer Explanations

1. D: Because the word *antibody* would likely come up in a biology class rather than everyday reading and is specific to a particular study, it is considered specialized. Choice A refers to simple and basic words that appear in daily speech, so it is incorrect. Choice B is incorrect because it is a type of vocabulary knowledge (meaning a student would recognize the word but not necessarily be able to use it correctly) rather than a type of vocabulary. Choice C is incorrect because although complicated words are more complex than basic words, they are not specialized.

2. A: Scaffolding, as a strategy, provides a framework (as scaffolding would for a structure) to enable building around a foundation. In this way, providing cultural references enables students to make connections and build on existing knowledge. Choice B is incorrect; collaborative learning in this regard refers to students working together to learn language and new vocabulary. Discourse refers to conversation with another student as another example of collaborative learning, so Choice C is incorrect. Finally, Choice D is incorrect. Relevance has more to do with the importance of the student's new culture and the knowledge they gain around vocabulary and understanding why it's important in the English language or American culture.

3. C: Morphemic analysis involves the breaking down of words into smaller parts that have meaning and using those meanings to put together enough information to understand the meaning of the larger word. Choice A is incorrect because contextual analysis requires that students look at the context of the word, how it's used, and sentence structures to learn the meaning through context. Etymological analysis, Choice B, refers to the history and origin of the full word or, sometimes, the root word itself, so it is incorrect. Choice D is incorrect because, like context, inferential analysis requires the student to infer what a word means based on the sentences around it and the overall meaning of the passage.

4. B: Dictionaries allow students to look up synonyms and help them understand those nuances. Choice A is incorrect because glossaries are not exhaustive. In other words, a glossary may not have the word a student is exploring or the word's synonym. Style manuals are related to grammar and usage rather than vocabulary, so Choice C is incorrect. Choice D is incorrect because spell-check provides spelling corrections and sometimes grammar corrections but is a limited tool when it comes to synonyms.

Reading Fluency and Comprehension

Components of Reading Fluency that Support Comprehension

Reading Fluency

Several factors influence a student's reading development skills. Students learn to read at varying ages. A student's background knowledge, first language acquisition, and family involvement in reading all affect a student's progress. Therefore, when to introduce fluency instruction cannot be determined merely by a student's age or grade level. Fluency instruction begins when a student can use basic decoding skills and can read 90% of connected text with accuracy. Routinely assessing a student's decoding and accuracy skills will help to determine when to begin fluency instruction.

Even if students don't yet display automaticity, modeling can be used to initially introduce fluency. Modeling demonstrates social norms of reading rate and prosody while building vocabulary, academic language, and background knowledge.

Practice, Guidance, and Feedback
Accuracy and reading rate are fundamental components of fluency, but it's important to remember that practice is an essential component of effective fluency instruction. When teachers provide daily opportunities for students to learn words and utilize word-analysis skills, accuracy and rate are likely to increase.

Oral reading accompanied by guidance and feedback from teachers, peers, and/or parents has been shown to significantly improve fluency. In order to be beneficial, such feedback needs to provide targeted and differentiated advice on areas where a student needs improvement. It's also recommended that teachers provide feedback that includes a variety of strategies.

Research-Based, Systematic, Explicit Strategies That Improve Fluency and Accuracy
Word-reading accuracy requires that students have a strong understanding of letter-sound correspondence and the ability to accurately blend the sounds together. Providing systematic, explicit instruction in phonemic awareness, phonics, and decoding skills will cultivate such accuracy. When students are readily able to identify high-frequency sight words, their accuracy improves. Therefore, instructors should provide ample opportunities to practice these words.

Research-Based, Systematic, Explicit Strategies That Improve Fluency and Reading Rate
Reading aloud has proven effective in strengthening reading fluency. Whisper-reading accompanied by teacher monitoring has also proven effective for students who don't yet display automaticity in their decoding skills. Timed reading of sight phrases or stories also improves fluency with respect to rate. During a **timed-reading** exercise, the number of words read in a given amount of time is recorded. Routinely administering timed readings and displaying the results in graphs and charts has been shown to increase student motivation.

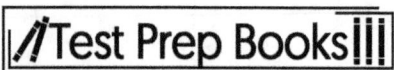

Timed-repeated readings, where a student reads and re-reads familiar texts in a given time, is a commonly used instructional strategy to increase reading speed, accuracy, and comprehension. Students read and re-read the passage until they reach their target rate.

Strategies that Improve Fluency and Prosody

Reading aloud not only improves the rate but also encourages appropriate expression, or **prosody**. When the teacher, the student, or an entire student body reads aloud, students become more exposed to the use of prosody; therefore, their reading expression is strengthened. When teachers read aloud, they model prosody, which cues students to the social norms of pace, pauses, inflection, emotion, and tone when reading different types of text. In **choral reading**, all students in the class read a passage aloud together, which allows them to hear text being read accurately and with good pacing and phrasing. By having students listen to recordings of themselves reading, teachers promote independent judgment and goal setting.

Reading theaters are another effective instructional practice that supports prosody. During reading theater instruction, students are assigned a character in a play. The emphasis is reading aloud with a purpose. Students use prosody to share their interpretations and understandings of their assigned characters' personalities and roles.

Phrase-cued reading is a third strategy that aids the development of prosody. During phrase-cued reading, teachers read a text aloud and mark where they pause or show intonation, emphasis, tone, inflections, and/or expression.

How to Address a Range of Needs

Several strategies can be implemented to assist English Language Learners, speakers of nonstandard English, advanced learners, and readers who have reading difficulties or disabilities. However, it's always important to provide each student with reading materials and strategies that are appropriate for their specific reading level and area of concern.

Struggling readers, students with reading difficulties or disabilities, and students with special needs benefit from direct instruction and feedback that teaches decoding and analysis of unknown words, automaticity in key sight words, and correct expression and phrasing. These learners also benefit from oral support. This may be provided through scaffolded reading, choral reading, partner reading, books on tape, and computer programs. Teachers should consistently offer opportunities for students to practice repeated reading, and should gradually introduce more challenging reading levels as students progress.

Providing ample opportunities to read orally with a scaffolding approach, which gradually increases the difficulty of the work and slowly asks for more independence from the student, also helps this group. For instance, teachers may read a short passage and have students immediately read it back to them. Direct instruction in English intonation patterns, syntax, and punctuation are effective tools in assisting English language learners with the development of prosody.

In order to broaden and enhance fluency for advanced learners, teachers should gradually introduce more advanced texts across several content areas.

Continued Assessment of Student Fluency

Assessment of fluency must include entry-level assessments, progress monitoring, and summative assessments of accuracy, rate, and prosody. The results should be analyzed and interpreted in order to

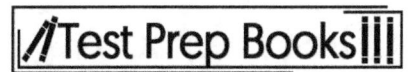

Reading Fluency and Comprehension

adjust instruction and provide struggling readers with proper interventions. Regular assessments also help teachers to construct differentiated instruction in order to address the fluency needs of advanced learners.

Assessing Students' Word-Reading Accuracy

Running records, a widely used fluency assessment, allows teachers to document error patterns in reading accuracy as students read benchmark books. As the student reads aloud, the teacher holds a copy of the same text and records any omissions, mispronunciations, and substitutions. With this information, teachers can determine which fluency strategies a student does or doesn't employ.

Using Timed Contextual Oral Reading to Assess Fluency and Rate

Assessment of reading rate often begins with sight-word reading automaticity. Automaticity assessment may also include the decoding of non-words in order to determine if a student is able to decode words using sound-syllable correspondence.

Among the most commonly used measurements of reading rate is oral contextual timed reading. During a **timed reading**, the number of errors made within a given amount of time is recorded. This data can be used to identify if a student's rate is improving and if reading rate falls within the recommended fluency rates for the student's grade level. If a student's reading rate is below average, any of the previously identified research-based, systematic, explicit strategies that improve fluency with respect to rate may be applied.

One common timed assessment for reading accuracy is the **WCPM**, the words-correct-per-minute assessment. The teacher presents an unfamiliar text to a student and asks the student to read aloud for one minute. As the student reads, the teacher records any omissions, mispronunciations, or substitutions. These errors are subtracted by the total number of words in the text to determine a score, which is then compared to oral reading fluency norms. With this assessment, teachers can select the appropriate level of text for each student.

Recommended Reading Fluency Rates		
Grade	**Semester**	**Correct Words Per Minute**
First Grade	Winter	38
	Spring	40–60
Second Grade	Fall	55
	Winter	73–79
	Spring	81–93
Third Grade	Fall	79
	Winter	83–92
	Spring	100–115
Fourth Grade	Fall	91–99

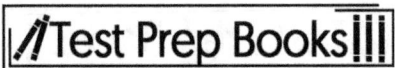

Recommended Reading Fluency Rates		
Grade	Semester	Correct Words Per Minute
	Winter	98–113
	Spring	106–119
Fifth Grade	Fall	105
	Winter	109–118
	Spring	118–128

<u>Assessing Prosody Through Observation of Connected-Text Reading</u>
In order to assess prosody, a teacher listens for inflection, expression, and pauses as the student reads a connected text aloud. The Integrate Reading Performance Record Oral Reading Fluency Scale designed by the National Assessment of Educational Progress (NAEP) is also used to assess prosody. Students at levels 3 and 4 are considered to be fluent with respect to prosody. Students at levels 1 and 2 are considered to be non-fluent in prosody.

- **Level 4:** Reads mainly in large phrase groups. The structure of the story is intact and the author's syntax is consistent, even if there are some deviations from the text. Most of the story is read with expression.

- **Level 3:** Reads mainly in three- or four-word phrase groups. Majority of phrasing is appropriate and preserves syntax of the author. Little expression is present with interpreting the text.

- **Level 2:** Reads two-word phrases with some three- or four-word groupings. Word-by-word reading may occur. Some word groupings may seem awkward and indicates the larger context is not being paid attention to.

- **Level 1:** Reads word-by-word. Some occasional two-or-three word phrases may be present, but they are not frequent or they don't preserve meaningful syntax.

Developing Fluent Reading and Comprehension

Independent Reading in the Development of Reading Comprehension and Fluency

Independent reading strategies promote healthy reading for pleasure and enjoyment. Hopefully, these strategies promote a lifelong love of reading. Students should be given daily, independent reading time in the classroom. Teachers phrase this time as **D.E.A.R.** or "Drop Everything and Read" time. Typically, this time can be incorporated into a teacher's reading block. It is suggested that students have about 20 minutes of D.E.A.R. time daily. Students can read a book from home, the library, or one selected from the variety of books found within the classroom.

Promoting Independent Reading

Teachers are required to have a classroom library. Some schools require a certain number of books or filled bookcases within a classroom. The library center should also contain more than just books. The classroom library should be an inviting environment for students. Small lamps make the area warmer—like home rather than school—and provide extra light for reading. Furniture—such as beanbag chairs, pillows, and small chairs—allow students to get comfortable, rather than reading at their desk. Not only is the environment important, but the reading center must also be an organized, designated space. If books are disorganized in the classroom library, students may be deterred from using the space appropriately, simply because they cannot find what they are looking for, or out of sheer frustration. Organizing books by theme or genre helps students search for the books they desire. For students in younger grades, books should be grouped in plastic tubs using picture and word category labels like "animals" or "holidays." This organization method is especially helpful to those learning to read.

A listening center is also another helpful space in the classroom library. In the listening center, students listen to stories that are played through a sound device (like a CD or MP3 player) and follow along in the text. A teacher can switch the book out weekly to match a theme in the classroom or they can leave a "free choice bin" for students to choose what they would like to listen to. Again, listening to the story will encourage and emphasize reading strategies, such as voice and pacing.

Having a bookshelf with the teacher's or students' text selections may encourage readers to select a good book quickly. Some students enjoy re-reading a book from a teacher read aloud; therefore, placing it in the "teacher's pick" area may encourage developing readers to pick it up. Students also like to follow their classmates. Therefore, teachers should have a section where students can place a book that they want to recommend to their friends. Older students can fill out brief recommendation sheets that briefly list a few of the book's main themes so that potential readers can see if they are interested in reading it. Reading from basal readers and school texts does not necessarily encourage reading for pleasure, as these texts are chosen by the school and instructor. For this reason, silent reading time is so important. Silent reading time gives students options and a chance to make their own choices. Students can choose the book and the appropriate reading pace when reading independently.

Comprehension and Analysis of Informational Texts

Teaching Students to Read Informational Texts

Here are some strategies for teaching students to understand and analyze informational texts.

Before the class reads a text, give students a few guiding questions and ask them to find the answers in the reading. For example, suppose that your students are about to read a book about the salmon lifecycle. You might ask them, "How many times do salmon travel during their lives?" and "Where do salmon die?" Approaching the text with guiding questions helps structure students' thoughts and teaches them to take notes. This method is particularly useful for young students, as it takes the attention off the unimportant details that sometimes fascinate young readers and redirects it to the central points of the text.

Teach students to summarize information. For example, you could ask students to take notes on the most important points in a text and then write a summary. Younger students do better with simple oral summaries, while older students can handle more complicated written work. Summarizing is a great way to improve comprehension. It also tests analysis skills, as students need to discern which points are important and which are just details.

Ask students to develop questions about the text. For instance, you could ask each student to read the assigned text and then bring one question about it to class. Teaching students to generate questions helps them be curious about reading and promotes creative thinking. This is particularly helpful when teaching older students to analyze more complex texts, as it teaches them to form arguments and evaluate material. For example, tenth graders could read a persuasive text and then bring questions that challenge its claims.

Teach students to form connections between the text and other material. For instance, students could read one book about Russia and another about Spain and then compare the two countries.

Alternatively, teachers can ask students to draw comparisons between the information in a text and their life experiences. This method is particularly effective for younger students, as it boosts engagement. For example, after reading a book about beavers, a teacher might ask their students whether any of them has seen a beaver. The class could then compare the information in the book to the students' experiences.

Independent and Reflective Reading

Students who engage in independent reading are able to read, retain, and analyze the text that they've read on their own, completely independent of outside aid. It also allows them to feel as if they've had a choice in picking their own text to read, instead of the feeling that it's been chosen for them. Reflective reading is the ability to absorb text with a sense of analysis in mind. Here are some examples of questions to ask while engaged in reflective reading:

- What am I reading?
- Why am I reading this?
- What is the author trying to tell me?
- Why is this character acting in a certain way?

Encouraging independent and reflective reading is dependent on the type of literature instructors choose to introduce to their classrooms. Culture, race, age, and reading level are all very important characteristics to keep in mind when choosing texts to have in the classroom for independent readers. If some students are ELLs, acquire some texts that are bilingual or ELL-appropriate. Choose authors with various ethnic backgrounds rather than the most popular books you find on an online blog. Find authors who have similar cultures to the students in the classroom. Choose difficult books for your advanced students and appropriate books for the students who still struggle with reading. Students will have a greater motivation to read and understand the language if they can relate to the message that's being delivered.

Comprehension and Analysis of Literary Texts

Teaching Literary Texts

While the strategies for teaching literary texts often overlap with those for teaching informational texts, there are a few key differences.

While guiding questions are just as helpful for literature as for informational texts, the questions for literary texts can be more open-ended and offer opportunities for students to express opinions on the reading. For example, teachers can ask questions like "Do you think the character makes the right decision?" or "How does the novel's setting contribute to the plot?" Teach students to engage with the material and back up their claims.

Teach students to support their analysis of literature with textual evidence. **Textual evidence** is material from the literary text itself. A student who bases an argument on historical facts, the author's life, or personal experience is not using textual evidence; however, someone who argues from the events and wording of a novel is using textual evidence. Teaching students about textual evidence helps them read closely and learn to form unbiased arguments.

Teach students to map stories and identify literary elements. **Freytag's pyramid** is the most common method of mapping the critical developments in a story. It is particularly useful for helping students understand the important events in a novel. For example, you could have students map *To Kill a Mockingbird* individually, and then discuss the maps as a class. Students should also know terms like "setting" and "theme" so that they can talk and write about their ideas.

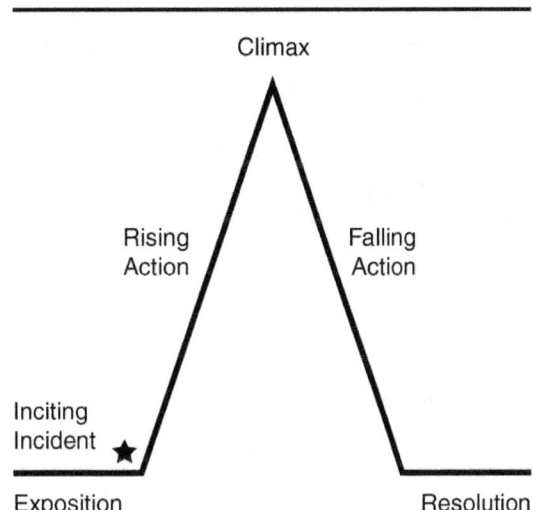

While there are correct and incorrect answers to questions about the factual events in a literary text, the answers to questions about themes and the text's message are not so simple. Instead of offering definitive readings on what the text means, facilitate discussion and make suggestions. Studying literature is a great way for students to develop creativity and argumentative skills, and you do not want to squelch that process by being too authoritative.

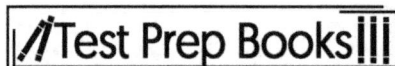

Metacognition and Critical Thinking

Teaching Metacognition and Critical Thinking

Metacognition is thinking about your own thoughts or learning process. For example, a student who thinks "When I think ___, I am making an assumption" is practicing metacognition. Metacognition is important because it enables people to evaluate their ideas objectively and determine whether they are valid. Metacognition can also help students think about the way they learn and improve their learning strategies. For example, a student who realizes that they can memorize things faster by writing them down can implement that technique to study efficiently.

Strategies for Developing Critical-Thinking Skills

Metacognitive strategies ask the student to decode text passages. In part, they require the student to preview text, be able to recognize unfamiliar words, then use context clues to define them for greater understanding. In addition, meta-cognitive strategies in the classroom employ skills such as being able to decode imagery, being able to predict, and being able to summarize. If a student can define unfamiliar vocabulary, make sense of an author's use of imagery, preview text prior to reading, predict outcomes during reading, and summarize the material, he or she is achieving effective reading comprehension. When approaching reading instruction, the teacher who encourages students to use phrases such as *I'm noticing*, *I'm thinking*, and *I'm wondering* is teaching a meta-cognitive type strategy.

Pre-Reading Strategies

Pre-reading strategies are important, yet often overlooked. Non-critical readers will often begin reading without taking the time to review factors that will help them understand the text. Skipping pre-reading strategies may result in a reader having to re-address a text passage more times than is necessary. Some pre-reading strategies include the following:

- Previewing the text for clues
- Skimming the text for content
- Scanning for unfamiliar words in context
- Formulating questions on sight
- Making predictions
- Recognizing the need for prior knowledge

Before reading a passage, a reader can enhance their ability to comprehend material by **previewing the text for clues.** This may mean making careful note of any titles, headings, graphics, notes, introductions, important summaries, and conclusions. It can involve a reader making physical notes regarding these elements or highlighting anything they think is important before reading. Often, a reader will be able to gain information just from these elements alone. Of course, close reading is required in order to fill in the details. A reader needs to be able to ask what they are reading about and what a passage is trying to say. The answers to these general questions can often be answered in previewing the text itself.

It's helpful to use pre-reading clues to determine the main idea and organization. First, any titles, sub-headings, and chapter headings should be read, and the test taker should make note of the author's credentials if any are listed. It's important to deduce what these clues may indicate as it pertains to the focus of the text and how it's organized.

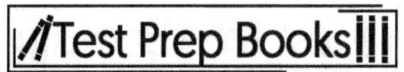

Reading Fluency and Comprehension

During pre-reading, readers should also take special note of how text features contribute to the central idea or thesis of the passage. Is there an index? Is there a glossary? What headings, footnotes, or other visuals are included and how do they relate to the details within the passage? Again, this is where any pre-reading notes come in handy, since a test taker should be able to relate supporting details to these textual features.

Next, a reader should **skim** the text for general ideas and content. This technique does not involve close reading; rather, it involves looking for important words within the passage itself. These words may have something to do with the author's theme. They may have to do with structure—for example, words such as *first, next, therefore*, and *last*. Skimming helps a reader understand the overall structure of a passage and, in turn, this helps them understand the author's theme or message.

From there, a reader should quickly *scan* the text for any unfamiliar words. When reading a print text, highlighting these words or making other marginal notation is helpful when going back to read text critically. A reader should look at the words surrounding any unfamiliar ones to see what contextual clues unfamiliar words carry. Being able to define unfamiliar terms through contextual meaning is a critical skill in reading comprehension.

A reader should also **formulate any questions** they might have before conducting close reading. Questions such as "What is the author trying to tell me?" or "Is the author trying to persuade my thinking?" are important to a reader's ability to engage critically with the text. Questions will focus a reader's attention on what is important in terms of main idea and supporting details.

Along with formulating questions, it is helpful to make predictions of what the answers to these questions and others will be. **Making predictions** involves using information from the text and personal experiences to make a thoughtful guess as to what will happen in the story and what outcomes can be expected.

Inferences refer to the ability to make logical assumptions based on contextual clues. People of all ages make inferences about the world around them on a daily basis but may not be aware of what they are doing. Even young children may infer that it is likely cold outside if they wake up and their bedroom is chilly or the floor is cold. While being driven somewhere on the highway and a child notices a person at the side of the road with a parked car, that child will likely infer that the individual is having car problems and is awaiting some assistance. Therefore, the challenge for educators is not necessarily teaching children how to infer, but rather demonstrating how this skill they already use can be transferred into the study of various texts.

The more initial practice children receive before moving into more complicated texts, the most success they will have in making accurate inferences and, in turn, the more fun they will have acting as text detectives.

Last, a reader should recognize that authors assume readers bring a **prior knowledge** set to the reading experience. Not all readers have the same experience, but authors seek to communicate with their readers. In turn, readers should strive to interact with the author of a particular passage by asking themselves what the passage demands they know during reading. This is also known as making a text-to-self connection. If a passage is informational in nature, a reader should ask "What do I know about this topic from other experiences I've had or other works I've read?" If a reader can relate to the content, they will better understand it.

Reading Fluency and Comprehension

All of the above pre-reading strategies will help the reader prepare for a closer reading experience. They will engage a reader in active interaction with the text by helping to focus the reader's full attention on the details that they will encounter during the next round or two of critical, closer reading.

Strategies During Reading

After pre-reading, a test taker can employ a variety of other reading strategies while conducting one or more closer readings. These strategies include the following:

- Clarifying during a close read
- Questioning during a close read
- Organizing the main ideas and supporting details
- Summarizing the text effectively

A reader needs to be able to **clarify** what they are reading. This strategy demands a reader think about how and what they are reading. This thinking should occur during and after the act of reading. For example, a reader may encounter one or more unfamiliar ideas during reading, then be asked to apply thoughts about those unfamiliar concepts after reading when answering test questions.

Questioning during a critical read is closely related to clarifying. A reader must be able to ask questions in general about what they are reading and about the author's supporting ideas. Questioning also involves a reader's ability to self-question. When closely reading a passage, it's not enough to simply try to understand the author. A reader must consider critical thinking questions to ensure they are comprehending intent. It's advisable, when conducting a close read, to write out margin notes and questions during the experience. These questions can be addressed later in the thinking process after reading and during the phase where a reader addresses the test questions. A reader who is successful in reading comprehension will iteratively question what they read, search text for clarification, then answer any questions that arise.

A reader should **organize** main ideas and supporting details cognitively as they read, as it will help them understand the larger structure at work. The use of quick annotations or marks to indicate what the main idea is and how the details function to support it can be helpful. Understanding the structure of a text passage is sometimes critical to answering questions about an author's approach, theme, messages, and supporting details. This strategy is most effective when reading informational or nonfiction texts. Texts that try to convince readers of a particular idea, that present a theory, or that try to explain difficult concepts are easier to understand when a reader can identify the overarching structure at work.

Post-Reading Strategies

After completing a text, a reader should be able to **summarize** the author's theme and supporting details in order to fully understand the passage. Being able to effectively restate the author's message, sub-themes, and pertinent, supporting ideas will help a reader gain an advantage when addressing standardized test questions.

A reader should also evaluate the strength of the predictions that were made in the pre-reading stage. Using textual evidence, predictions should be compared to the actual events in the story to see if the two were similar or not. Employing all of these strategies will lead to fuller, more insightful reading comprehension.

Critical Thinking

Critical thinking is a broad term that refers to students' ability to evaluate materials and form logical conclusions. For example, a student who reads a Shakespeare play and analyzes it is thinking critically; however, a student who identifies Shakespeare as the author is just stating a fact, not thinking critically.

Here are some techniques that you can use to help your students develop metacognition and critical thinking.

- When students pose an opinion, ask them why they have that opinion. For example, ask, "You've said that you really disliked the novel. Why do you think you feel that way?" This technique provides a way for students to learn to think through their own thought process. However, teachers should be wary of asking too many questions; if students have to defend every single opinion, they will become frustrated.

- Model metacognition by talking through your own thought processes. For example, you might write textual evidence on the board and then map your thoughts as you analyze it.

- Ask students about how they experience learning, and encourage them to use their observations to study more efficiently. For example, you could ask your students to think about whether they are more visual or auditory learners, and then ask them to brainstorm ways that they could use their strengths to learn new vocabulary words.

- Teach your students to identify logical fallacies. A **fallacy** is a way of using logic poorly, which may result in a false conclusion. For example, the claim that "Dickens criticizes the government, so he must be an anarchist" contains a fallacy because it presents a false dilemma: wholeheartedly supporting the government and being an anarchist are not the only possible viewpoints.

Discussions of Literary and Informational Print and Nonprint Texts

Fostering Evidence-Based Collaborative Discussions

Two great ways to engage students in discussion are literature circles and discussion circles. Literature circles are groups of students who read the same text independently and meet to discuss their findings. Depending on the needs of your class, you may choose to assign books to your groups or allow them to choose their own.

Recall that discussion circles are similar to literature circles, but they focus on discussing a topic rather than the text itself. Depending on your students' age and ability, you can guide the discussion to be about anything from basic facts (for example, summarizing what happened in a text) to abstract ideas (for example, discussing the themes of a novel). For example, after reading *Huckleberry Finn*, students may discuss the immorality of slavery.

Debates are also a good way for students to practice building convincing arguments. Teachers can break the class into groups and have them prepare arguments supporting contradictory claims. For example, students could divide into a group arguing that *Jane Eyre* is a feminist novel, and another arguing that it is not. Depending on your topic and how popular each viewpoint is, you can allow students to choose their side or assign them randomly. Having students argue for the side they do not believe builds objectivity and critical thinking, so it is not an inferior option.

Practice Quiz

1. Which of the following terms refers to techniques that allow students to progress toward a greater level of understanding on an increasingly independent level?
   a. Discourse
   b. Differentiation
   c. Scaffolding
   d. Benchmarking

2. Which of the following statements about literacy development is true?
   a. Research shows that literacy development begins as early as 3 months of age.
   b. Between 3 months and 6 months, babies begin to study a speaker's mouth and listen closely to speech sounds.
   c. Between 6 months and 9 months, babies can generally recognize a growing number of commonly repeated words, utter simple words, respond appropriately to simple requests, and begin to attempt to group sounds.
   d. Between 9 months and 12 months, babies rapidly strengthen their communication skills, connecting sounds to meanings and combining sounds to create coherent sentences.

3. Receptive language development refers to which of the following stages of literacy?
   a. Beginning literacy
   b. Early intermediate literacy
   c. Intermediate literacy
   d. Early advanced literacy

4. All EXCEPT which of the following are considered non-decodable sight words?
   a. None
   b. Who
   c. Runner
   d. Said

5. While studying vocabulary, a student notices that the words *circumference*, *circumnavigate*, and *circumstance* all begin with the prefix *circum–*. The student uses her knowledge of affixes to infer that all of these words share what related meaning?
   a. Around, surrounding
   b. Travel, transport
   c. Size, measurement
   d. Area, location

See answers on the next page.

Answer Explanations

1. C: *Scaffolding* refers to techniques that allow students to progress toward a greater level of understanding on an increasingly independent level by incrementally increasing difficulty and independence. *Discourse* is a general term that refers to oral or written communication, so Choice A is incorrect. *Differentiation* refers to tailoring instructional methods and activities towards individual students or different levels. Therefore, Choice B is incorrect. Choice D is incorrect because *benchmarking* refers to setting measurable standards during the learning process.

2. B: Choice B is a correct statement about the generally accepted progression of normal literacy development. Choice A is incorrect because research indicates that literacy development begins from birth, and that from birth to 3 months of age, babies start recognizing the sounds of familiar voices, and this actually begins the early stages of literacy development. Choices C and D are incorrect because those skills start developing a bit later than stated, between 9 months and 12 months of age for Choice C, and in the toddler years for Choice D.

3. A: Receptive language development is a term used to describe the beginning literacy stage, during which children begin understanding the "input" of language. This means that they start developing the ability to connect words with their meanings and comprehend spoken language that others say or read.

4. C: The word runner is a decodable word because it follows the rules of phonics and is spelled phonetically. The other three choices are considered non-decodable sight words that students simply need to memorize because they are not spelled phonetically.

5. A: The affix *circum–* originates from Latin and means "around" or "surrounding". It is also related to other words that indicate something round, such as *circle* and *circus*.

Reading Program Development

Involving Stakeholders, Including Caregivers, in Reading Initiatives

A **stakeholder** is a person who has an interest in or is affected by something within an organization. For example, if Adam's son goes to Maple Academy, Adam has a vested interest in that school and is therefore a stakeholder in Maple Academy. Stakeholders in schools include parents, teachers, school administrators, board members, government officials who make polices about education, and the community as a whole. While not every stakeholder will be involved in the school to the same degree, engaging stakeholders in reading initiatives will create an environment that fosters student success.

Here are some ways to involve stakeholders in reading initiatives.

- Create a supportive environment where school staff can share experiences and ideas. For example, staff could have a monthly coffee meetup to exchange stories about what has and hasn't worked in their classrooms. By swapping knowledge, teachers can learn effective teaching techniques and avoid repeating others' mistakes.

- Regularly communicate your progress and goals with all stakeholders. For example, you might start a monthly newsletter and make it available to all parents and community members. By maintaining communication with your stakeholders, you can encourage them to contribute to your program in various ways. For example, community members could fundraise to buy more books, or parents could come and read with students in class.

- When possible, partner with organizations and individuals to expand the reading culture in your community. For example, a school could partner with a local library to hold a reading challenge and offer prizes to students who read a certain number of books. Other ideas include asking a business to subsidize an essay contest about a topic that relates to the company, and asking community members who are involved in writing or publishing to visit the class.

Increasing Caregiver Involvement in Reading Education

Here are some strategies that you can use to help your students' caregivers engage in reading education.

Educate caregivers on reading techniques and offer them resources for teaching at home. For example, you could host workshops on teaching phonics so that caregivers know how to help their children sound out words when reading at home. Suggesting supplemental resources for both parents and students is also a great idea. Parents can benefit from recommendations of literacy activities, books to read with their children, or books and websites that teach them how to help their students succeed in reading.

Make opportunities for caregivers to join your classroom. For example, you could have parents come and read aloud to students in class; alternatively, you could invite caregivers who work in fields that relate to your reading to come and answer questions. When parents spend time in the classroom, they gain a better understanding of their child's abilities and needs. Classroom involvement may also inspire caregivers to spend more time working with their children at home.

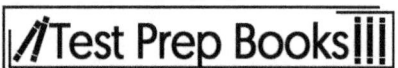

Communicate regularly with caregivers. Newsletters, parent/teacher meetings, and meetings where the teacher meets with both the parent and the student are all useful. Communication regarding the class's progress and children's individual needs gives caregivers the information they need to help their students succeed. Communication also encourages caregivers to take an active part in their children's education.

Promoting Family and Community Involvement in Literacy Activities

The following are strategies for promoting purposeful and independent reading of a wide variety of texts:

- Promote independent reading of narrative, literary, expository, and informational texts.
- Teach students how to select books that are at appropriate reading levels.
- Use students' personal interests to help motivate them to read independently.
- Provide structured reading opportunities in class.
- Encourage independent reading at home.
- Monitor students' independent reading.

In addition to teacher read-alouds, as discussed earlier, students should have approximately twenty minutes per day to read independently. This time should be structured and occur at predictable times each day or throughout the week. Students should be encouraged to read a variety of texts at this time (narrative, literary, expository, and informational texts). Students also should read independently.

In order to benefit from independent reading, students must read texts that are appropriate for their assessed reading level. Therefore, students should be aware of their reading levels and be able to select texts that coincide with this level. For students in primary school, the **five-finger test** can be used in the text-selection process. The five-finger test asserts that if a student has trouble with five or more words on a randomly selected page, then the book is above that student's reading level. For older readers, the teacher can group texts into levels and/or categories, from which students can select based on their personal interests.

In order for independent reading time to be effective, students should be accountable for what is read. A great assessment tool is to have each student give an oral report of one book that they have read during the marking period. Students should be given nightly reading homework as well. Teachers may require students to log the number of minutes read each night. Such reading logs should require parents to sign next to the number of minutes a night a child has read.

Reading Policies, Program Information, and Assessment Data

Relevant Research Findings

As a reading specialist instructor, it is important to not only educate students but also to further the knowledge base of other teachers and educators. New research on learning disabilities, teaching techniques, and even psychological research is very valuable to any educational institution. This new information will impact the overall instruction of students throughout departments and potentially influence funding opportunities. Because research is constantly producing new ideas and improvements, educational institutions that incorporate it will continue their strive toward excellence. Therefore, it is important to offer the highest quality of information possible.

New information is only as good as its quality and authenticity. It is important to investigate all new research carefully, and make sure the sources are credible. Assessing the findings and claims of other professionals is important as well. If the information doesn't make sense or is poorly documented, reading specialists should consider researching the same material from a different source. When drawing from official research documentation, one must check bibliographies or specific incidents mentioned to fact-check the writer's claims. Not only does this new research impact the individual reading specialist, but also the students and the institution's integrity. Reading specialists must also be aware of trends within the research and whether the research in question is attempting to support a specific agenda or theory. Being mindful of opposing viewpoints in research topics will enable a reading instructor to offer balanced information that addresses topics.

Educational research can be quite difficult to understand and apply. When presenting information to peers, the specialist must use clear language and be prepared to address questions. Being able to present this material necessitates more than just knowledge of the research; one must be able to apply it to the current programs, or at least present ideas on how to do so. Reading instructors should ask themselves: Can this research help address current program issues? Can this research accelerate or improve student learning? Can these methodologies be seamlessly integrated, or will there be problems adjusting program parameters? Such analysis will not only determine whether the research in question has good information but also whether it's appropriate for the current needs of the school, faculty, and students.

Communicating with Policymakers, the Media, and the General Public

Advocating for positive change and support of literacy is an essential role of reading specialists. Essentially, this means educating the public and key figures in society about the importance of reading education in order to garner support for programs within the school as well as research. It is through advocacy by educators and other experts that people become aware of key issues within education and are moved to aid instructors in their mission to enhance the lives of students through literacy. Instructors can do this in several ways, but primarily it is through speaking engagements with other people.

Some of the most important people to seek advocacy from are elected officials and policymakers who establish rules and regulations of state and county education. These individuals can range from senators, governors, and even members of the State Departments of Education. These people are elected to serve the best interest of their constituents, so it is the job of the reading specialist to show how reading education efforts are in the people's interest. This can be done by presenting research on how reading impacts child development and career opportunities. Instructors can also highlight their own work within the classroom, sharing the accomplishments of individual students. Instructors can also write letters to officials or attend official school board events to promote key programs.

The public is also important to enhancing education. After all, it's the public who ultimately elects policymakers and controls the rules of the land. Advocating how reading and literacy empower children to reach their potential is an important step in gaining the attention needed to make valuable change for education. Community support is also what will help create fundraisers and similar events needed to raise school funding for programs and structural projects. The public might not know a lot about the role of literacy in early development, so sharing information on the subject will demonstrate that their investment in education is well funded. Engaging with the public also helps parents and family members

be aware of learning issues and can open up dialogues that will lead to more children receiving valuable resources and instruction.

Presenting one's voice in the media will also gain advocacy, whether through writing or commenting on Web articles or sharing views on literacy through social media. Web networking is a great way to tell people on a grand scale how important reading education is for America's youths. Instructors and literacy advocates should not be afraid to address issues by commenting on video or written posts that seem to be contrary to educational values. Instructors should also encourage other staff to be active online, sharing their knowledge and passion for education.

Partnerships Between Schools and Community Agencies

As mentioned, advocating literacy is highly important to sustaining the value and role of education throughout the country. To this extent, no one can enhance educational programs alone. Schools are tied to the communities they are a part of, so it is through generous funding and support from community agencies that schools are able to continue their impact on education. Therefore, cultivating partnerships between local schools and the community is essential on many levels. Not only will this help gain support for key programs, it also serves to get parents and key community figures involved in the education process.

Being proactive in the community will help when seeking which groups may be interested in collaboration. Reading specialists should look for partners that share similar values, such as promoting reading, education, or outreach. Common places where people gather, such as a community gym or even a theater company, are ideal because both depend on the community being proactive and prosperous. For example, an independent theater company is a great place to promote literacy programs because plays are both a dramatic and written art form. Organizing a collaborative partnership could bring positive attention to both groups. The students' program would be highlighted and garner support, while the theater company would gain more attention, not only for their performances but also for giving back to the community. Partnerships can be established by any kind of agency, from local charities to large or small businesses.

Connecting with the community is key; one has to engage potential partners in order to assess whether a collaboration can even be possible. Maintaining contact lists will enable the reading specialists to have a pool of potential groups to reach out to and partner with at all times. It is also important to have a clear form of collaboration in place. Will the partner in question sponsor an event, hand out pamphlets on the importance of reading, or host a field trip? Planning collaborative efforts in advance is essential to both parties.

Comprehensive Reading and Reading Intervention Programs

Choosing Reading Materials and Curricula

When choosing curricula to use in your classroom, there are a number of factors to consider.

Consider the needs of your students, and choose materials that will accommodate those needs. For example, if you are teaching a group of students who are repeating a year because they struggled to learn reading, find materials that offer plenty of resources for struggling learners and children with learning disabilities. Alternatively, if you are teaching gifted students, you need a curriculum that is fast-paced and activities that will allow students to explore their individual interests.

Find materials that offer flexibility for the teacher and students. For example, a good curriculum will offer ideas on alternative teaching materials, assessment strategies, and activities so that teachers can tailor the materials to the needs of their class. Having a flexible curriculum also allows you to modify the level of your materials for students who are above and below the average level in your class.

Make sure that the materials you choose are clear and appealing to students. Avoid choosing curriculum with unclear explanations. You should also make sure that your materials do not include elements that will confuse students or distract them from learning the material, such as outdated language or disorienting formatting. Finally, the reading materials should be interesting so that students are motivated to read and learn from their studies.

Ensure that your materials integrate well with any assessments you have planned. For example, if your school requires a certain test at winter break, make sure that you will cover the materials your students will be tested on before the exam.

Criteria to Determine the Effectiveness of Reading Programs

Determining the Effectiveness of Reading Materials

You can predict whether materials will be effective by looking at a number of factors.

Make sure that the materials you choose are consistent with current research on reading. Keeping up with current research will prevent you from using outdated curricula, and it will make you aware of new and improved teaching methods. However, the newest methods are not always the best. Instead of trying to incorporate every trending idea, look for materials that use methods that are backed by a wide body of research.

Consider whether the materials offer a balanced approach to reading instruction. You should choose materials that teach all reading skills well instead of focusing unduly on some while ignoring others. For example, a bad curriculum might focus on vocabulary and reading speed so much that it neglects to teach students phonics. A good curriculum, however, teaches basic skills like phonics while also incorporating vocabulary, comprehension exercises, and writing skills.

Look at the lesson sequence and consider whether the material is organized in a way that is conducive to learning. For example, a bad program might start teaching complex phonograms (like "sh" as in "ship") before it has finished teaching basic consonants (like "s" and "h"). This design would make it difficult for students to learn, because they would have to recognize letters in phonograms before they recognized them in isolation. A good program will organize the material so that students grasp fundamental concepts before encountering more complex ones.

Improving Curriculum Content and Instruction

Evaluating Data to Improve Curricula

Here are some concepts that can help teachers interpret school data and program evaluation results.

- Use assessments to identify your class's strengths and weaknesses. For example, your students might have a high average in reading, but a low average in writing. This information would suggest that you should keep using the program and techniques that you have been using to teach reading, but you should try new materials and strategies for writing instruction.

- Compare your class's data with the data from the school and the whole state. By identifying shared characteristics, you can deduce which elements of your program are hindering and which are helping. For example, you might find that your class has low spelling scores, but your coworker's class has high scores in the area. If you are using different curricula but similar teaching methods, you can deduce that you need to implement better materials. In a similar way, you might find that both your school and state have low scores in writing, and you can infer that the state curriculum is weak in that area and could use supplementation.

- If possible, go over assessment results with your coworkers. Offering each other thoughts from an outsider's perspective may help you approach your program more objectively and think of new ideas.

Once you understand your program's strengths and weaknesses, you can move on to modifying your materials. Here are some tips for adjusting your program.

- Do not be afraid to cobble two or more programs together. For example, you may find that your current approach teaches reading and writing well but is not good at teaching reading comprehension. Instead of trying an entirely new program, you could keep the elements that are working in your current approach and simply introduce reading comprehension materials from a different program.

- Be creative and experiment with your materials and your teaching techniques. You can switch the genres, activities, or delivery methods that you are using. Program modifications are not set in stone; if you try a new technique and find that it does not work, you can always change course! You can only find what works well for your students by experimenting with different methods.

- Keep assessing to make sure that your modifications are working. For example, you might want to test your students two weeks after implementing a new strategy so that you can determine whether or not it is working.

Collaborating with Others to Assist in Reading Instruction

Using Assistants in Reading Instruction

There are several roles for people who assist teachers in the classroom. **Paraprofessionals** (sometimes called teacher assistants or instructional aides) are trained staff members who help teachers manage the class's behavior and support learners. For example, aides often help students who have physical or learning disabilities by working with them individually. Paraprofessionals may also address behavior issues so that the teacher does not have to interrupt class. **Tutors** fill a similar role, but they do not usually handle classroom management. Instead, they work with students in small groups or individually, either in class or outside class. For example, a tutor might give English lessons to ESL students while the rest of the class works with the teacher. Finally, **volunteers** are parents and community members who are not trained to work in the classroom; they help the teacher with easy tasks, such as reading to students.

Here are some ways you can support and coach the paraprofessionals and other helpers in your classroom:

Make sure that you are not assigning your classroom helpers tasks that they are not allowed to do. For example, paraprofessionals are only allowed to teach under the direct supervision of a teacher. Therefore, a teacher who asked their aide to design and teach a lesson independently would be acting inappropriately. Teachers are the ones responsible for their class; while they can certainly ask their assistants to help them in a limited capacity, they should not hoist the responsibility for teaching onto paraprofessionals.

Set aside dedicated time to training paraprofessionals, aides, and other people who are helping in your classroom. For example, if you have a student-teacher in your class, take time to give them mini-lessons on the teaching techniques that you are using in class. Taking time to teach your paraprofessionals and other helpers helps both parties; your assistants learn how to offer high-quality support in the classroom, and you will have an easier time managing your class because of their help.

Model good teaching practices to show assistants how to teach effectively. For example, you might coach paraprofessionals by having them watch you teach a concept, and then having them teach it back to you. Simply observing you teach in class is also helpful, particularly for volunteers or trainees who are not yet familiar with teaching methods.

Make sure that you communicate your needs clearly and listen to your assistants. You should never simply assume that classroom helpers know where they are needed. Communicate about daily issues, such as telling helpers who to help. This could include sitting down to talk about class progress and concerns about particular students. Because they spend more time observing the class instead of focusing on teaching, paraprofessionals and aides often have valuable insights into student behavior and teaching effectiveness.

Addressing the Goals of the Reading Program

Teaching is inherently a collaborative process. In addition to working with students and learning together as a class, a reading specialist can seek assistance from fellow staff and involve individual families with their child's education. Working with community figures can also broaden a reading specialist's skill set while enhancing their ability to provide high-quality, well-rounded instruction.

Being a reading specialist on staff at school doesn't isolate the individual to one classroom or a single subject. Quite the opposite. While a reading instructor has a central education focus, their insight on reading and communication learning can benefit teachers in many other departments. For example, if a math teacher has a student struggling with a particular concept, a reading instructor can offer advice on how to assess where communication disconnects may lie. The issue may be related to math, but the reading instructor can still work with the math instructor and explain the concept in a different way. On the other hand, a reading instructor can benefit from the different methods of content instruction or assessment practices used by other instructors. Collaborating with other teachers enables the reading specialist to basically assist not only students in their classroom but students in other classes. Teaching staff should be seen as a team with the shared goal and responsibility of providing students with great education in all of their subjects.

Like working with fellow teachers, a reading instructor should also feel comfortable reaching out to administrative staff, the community, and parents for support. Because the instructor can't be everywhere at once, these people are key for providing valuable insight on individual students and also helping them with their education outside of class. School administrative professionals can provide information on behavioral issues or give feedback on a student's communication/interactions that can help instructors isolate core issues and adjust instruction. Parents can do this also, but because they are at home with the student, they can actually reinforce teaching methods for homework. This, in turn, will lead to more support and a concentrated effort from the parents to assist their children with everyday writing and communication scenarios too, providing additional lessons outside of the classroom. On a grander scale, community events are a great way for students to listen to proper language and practice applying their language skills in real-world scenarios.

Practice Quiz

1. When selecting books for independent reading, parents should help students identify appropriate books by doing which of the following?
    a. Providing their own favorite book so they can discuss it
    b. Selecting what is available at home
    c. Using the five-finger test
    d. Choosing unfamiliar topics to explore

2. A teacher who regularly introduces brand-new instructional methods in a classroom is doing which of the following?
    a. Potentially damaging the integrity of instruction
    b. Demonstrating investment in their field
    c. Encouraging students to seek out new strategies
    d. Using differentiating instruction

3. A reading teacher who partners with a local library for a reading program is doing which of the following?
    a. Abdicating responsibility
    b. Engaging school administrators
    c. Expanding community reading culture
    d. Influencing policymakers

4. Which one of the following is NOT an effective tool for independent reading?
    a. Accountability
    b. Five-finger test
    c. Nonfiction only
    d. Structured time

See answers on the next page.

Answer Explanations

1. C: The five-finger test means that if a text has more than five words on a page that a student is unfamiliar with, the book is above their grade level and is therefore not appropriate. This test is a good way to select books for independent reading and ensure they are at the right reading level. Choice *A* is incorrect. Although being able to discuss a story with a child is great, students may not be interested in the text, or parental favorites may not be at grade level, making them a poor choice. Choice *B* is incorrect. Availability matters, but as with parental choices, it doesn't ensure the book is an appropriate selection for a student. Finally, Choice *D* is incorrect because a student is more likely to engage in independent reading if they are interested in the topic. Unfamiliar topics may not pique a student's interest and impact motivation.

2. A: Often new instructional methods are exciting but must be fully vetted prior to being introduced in a classroom environment. Further, regularly introducing new methods and strategies may be confusing for students whose reading skills benefit from consistent methods that are backed by significant research. Choice *B* is incorrect. Investment in the educational field is certainly important, but research is regularly producing new ideas, and an invested educator is fully vetting new methods as they understand the value of using methods that are tested and balanced with the needs of the students. Choice *C* is incorrect as well. Again, regularly introducing methods may be confusing to students and may, in fact, teach them the opposite. Finally, Choice *D* is incorrect. Differentiating instruction means tailoring strategies to individual student needs rather than teaching a different method or strategy when it is introduced to the field.

3. C: Partnering on reading initiatives with local organizations that have community access and influence helps expand a culture of reading in a community. As a result, students will value reading as well. Choice *A* is incorrect. Part of a reading specialist's or teacher's responsibility is to influence not just their students but the environments in which their students learn. That means engaging with parents, stakeholders, caregivers, and communities. Choice *B* is incorrect. Although a teacher might need to confer with an administrator for such a program, it likely would not involve them as much as it would the teacher/specialist and the library/organization itself. Choice *D* is incorrect because this initiative might be seen by policymakers but is not, in itself, the kind of lobbying effort (such as speaking at a city council meeting) that would influence a policymaker.

4. C: Independent reading is most effective when students are reading a variety of texts, including fiction and nonfiction. Choice *A* is incorrect because accountability is important whether it's through an oral or written book report. Ensuring that students are following through on this initiative is key to building their confidence as independent readers. Choice *B* is incorrect; the five-finger test is an important tool in ensuring that the books a student selects are appropriate for their grade level. Choice *D* is incorrect because setting aside time for independent reading gives it value and also gives a student time to complete the activity (in case there is minimal time for it at home or it is not prioritized there).

Practice Test

1. A graphic organizer is a method of achieving what?
    a. Integrating knowledge and ideas
    b. Generating questions
    c. Determining point of view
    d. Determining the author's purpose

2. Nursery rhymes are used in kindergarten to develop what?
    a. Print awareness
    b. Phoneme recognition
    c. Syllabication
    d. Structural analysis

3. What nonfiction texts can be used to teach reading standards?
    I. United States documents
    II. Magazines for pleasure
    III. Science and social studies textbooks

    a. III only
    b. II and III
    c. I and III
    d. I, II, and III

4. Timed oral reading can be used to assess which of the following?
    a. Phonics
    b. Listening comprehension
    c. Reading rate
    d. Background knowledge

5. Which is NOT a reason why independent reading is important for developing reading comprehension?
    a. It helps students develop a lifelong love of reading.
    b. It encourages students to read a genre they enjoy.
    c. It provides an opportunity for students to read at their own pace.
    d. It gives students time to visit the reading corner, which is an area of the classroom that is restful and enjoyable.

6. It is important to choose a variety of texts to elicit higher-level thinking skills. Which of the following text groupings would be appropriate to reach this goal?
    a. Basal readers, fantasy texts, and sci-fi novels
    b. Nonfiction, fiction, cultural pieces, and United States documents
    c. Scholastic magazine articles
    d. Textbooks and high-interest blogs

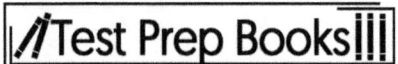

7. To thoroughly assess students' phonics skills, teachers should administer assessments that require students to do which of the following?
    a. Decode in context only
    b. Decode in isolation only
    c. Both A and B are correct
    d. Neither A nor B

8. Print awareness includes all EXCEPT which of the following concepts?
    a. The differentiation of uppercase and lowercase letters
    b. The identification of word boundaries
    c. The proper tracking of words
    d. The spelling of sight words

9. What type of writing is detached, to the point, and usually written in the second person point of view?
    a. Persuasive
    b. Expository
    c. Narrative
    d. Argumentative

10. What is a phoneme?
    a. A word
    b. A relationship between a letter and a sound
    c. An individual sound
    d. A consonant

11. Why are intervention groups important to advanced learners?
    a. They are not useful, as they do not need intervention in a particular skill.
    b. They can be used to teach struggling students.
    c. They can be given more advanced and complex work.
    d. They can be given tasks to do in the classroom while others are meeting for intervention.

12. The identification of morphemes within words occurs during the instruction of what?
    a. Structural analysis
    b. Syllabic analysis
    c. Phonics
    d. The alphabetic principle

13. What is Freytag's pyramid?
    a. A way of structuring goals for the class
    b. A way of organizing class time
    c. A way of mapping the plot of a story
    d. A way of mapping the relationships between characters in a story

14. Poetry is often an effective device when teaching what skill?
    a. Fluency
    b. Spelling
    c. Writing
    d. Word decoding

15. Which of the following is NOT the best way to utilize a reading center or corner in a classroom?
    a. As a spot for students to play games
    b. As a private and quiet place to chat about books
    c. As a location to provide a variety of leveled readers
    d. As fun and entertaining décor to enhance a comfortable learning environment

16. A student spells *eagle* as *EGL*. This student is performing at which stage of spelling?
    a. Conventional
    b. Phonetic
    c. Semiphonetic
    d. Transitional

17. Structural analysis would be the most appropriate strategy in determining the meaning of which of the following words?
    a. Extra
    b. Improbable
    c. Likely
    d. Wonder

18. A teacher has two groups of students. One group is instructed to complete the reading and write down any words they do not know. The other group is provided with a list of vocabulary words to define prior to the reading. The group provided with the list is most likely struggling with which of the following?
    a. Spelling
    b. Automaticity
    c. Dictionary use
    d. Comprehension

19. Which statement about choosing a reading program for learner-centered education is true?
    a. Use older materials because they have been tested by numerous teachers.
    b. Use a program that offers options so that you can tailor the program to your students.
    c. Never blend two programs, as it makes things confusing for the students.
    d. Use the program that the other teachers in your school are using.

20. What is a fallacy?
    a. A misuse of logic
    b. A false conclusion to a logical argument
    c. An incorrect fact
    d. A sign that a source is not reliable

21. Barbara wants to create an information-rich environment for her students. Which measures should she take?
    a. Building a diverse classroom library, decorating the classroom, and integrating technology with her lessons
    b. Building a diverse classroom library, avoiding technology in the classroom
    c. Removing non-essential books from the classroom, using exclusively non-print materials
    d. Using technology in the classroom and avoiding distractions by not decorating the classroom

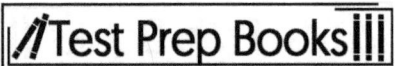

22. How are typographic features useful when teaching reading comprehension?
    a. Typographic features are graphics used to illustrate the story and help students visualize the text.
    b. Typographic features give the answers in boldfaced print.
    c. Typographic features are not helpful when teaching reading comprehension and should not be used.
    d. Typographic features such as boldface, italics, and subheadings can be used to highlight important vocabulary or content or indicate changes in topics.

23. Which statement about sight words is true?
    a. Sight words are always taught before any other reading skill.
    b. Sight words were popular in the 1940s.
    c. Sight words are usually short, common words.
    d. Sight words are no longer used in modern teaching.

24. Why is annotating texts a beneficial exercise for students?
    a. It teaches them to think independently.
    b. It helps them learn to identify key points.
    c. It teaches them to write faster.
    d. It helps shy students engage in discussion.

25. Which task should a teacher NOT assign to their teaching aide?
    a. Scoring multiple choice tests
    b. Teaching a class
    c. Working individually with struggling students
    d. Telling disruptive students to be quiet during a lesson

26. What is the role of a reading specialist position at a school site?
    I. To inform staff of changes in the curriculum
    II. To offer reading lessons in the classroom
    III. To instruct staff on how to do their job

    a. II only
    b. I and II
    c. II and III
    d. I, II, and III

27. A teacher is looking for ways to expand her students' vocabulary. Which of the following is an effective strategy to encourage independent word learning?
    a. Pre-teaching words to the class before reading a text
    b. Having students pair up to read a story
    c. Teaching students to use a dictionary
    d. Assigning extra essays for homework

28. Laura plans to test her students at the first of the year. She wants to assess specific skills to find out if students have any weaknesses that they need to work on. Which kind of assessment should Laura use?
    a. Screening assessment
    b. Diagnostic assessment
    c. Progress monitoring assessment
    d. Outcomes assessment

29. Phonological awareness is best assessed through which of the following?
    a. Identification of rimes or onsets within words
    b. Identification of letter-sound correspondences
    c. Comprehension of an audio book
    d. Writing samples

30. The study of roots, suffixes, and prefixes is called what?
    a. Listening comprehension
    b. Word consciousness
    c. Word morphology
    d. Textual analysis

31. A student can read and comprehend a text with about 80% accuracy. What is the level of this text according to the Informal Reading Inventory?
    a. Independent level
    b. Hearing capacity level
    c. Frustration level
    d. Instructional level

32. Effective writing instruction involves all but which of the following?
    a. Feedback
    b. Revision
    c. Vocabulary
    d. Prewriting

33. A teacher wants to encourage a better connection with the text and facilitate complex discussions about themes and ideas. Which strategy would she use with her students?
    a. Literature circle
    b. Jigsaw discussions
    c. Discussion circle
    d. Role-play

34. What is the alphabetic principle?
    a. The understanding that letters represent sounds in words
    b. The ability to combine letters to correctly spell words
    c. The proper use of punctuation within writing
    d. The memorization of all the letters in the alphabet

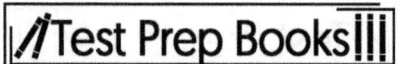

35. When differentiating phonics instruction for English-language learners (ELLs), teachers should do which of the following?
    a. Increase the rate of instruction.
    b. Begin with the identification of word boundaries.
    c. Focus on syllabication.
    d. Capitalize on the transfer of relevant skills from the learners' original language(s).

36. Which award is given to children's books?
    a. The Newberry Medal
    b. The Young Reader Engagement Prize for Excellence in Literature
    c. The Sundance Award
    d. All of the above

37. Jasmine wants to improve her reading program. In which order should she proceed?
    a. Assess students, modify the program, identify weaknesses, experiment with different techniques, reassess students.
    b. Modify the program, assess students, identify weaknesses, reassess students, experiment with different techniques.
    c. Assess students, identify weaknesses, modify the program, experiment with different techniques, reassess students.
    d. Experiment with different techniques, assess students, modify the program, identify weaknesses, reassess students.

38. What is "text evidence" when referring to answering a comprehension question?
    a. Taking phrases directly from the text itself to answer a question
    b. Using a variety of resources to find the answer
    c. Using technology and websites to locate an answer
    d. Paraphrasing and using a student's own words to answer the question

39. Which trait is most commonly associated with giving individuality and style to writing?
    a. Voice
    b. Word choice
    c. Presentation
    d. Ideas

40. What allows readers to effectively translate print into recognizable speech?
    a. Fluency
    b. Spelling
    c. Phonics
    d. Word decoding

41. What kind of assessments are most beneficial for students with special needs?
    a. Frequent and ongoing
    b. Weekly
    c. Monthly
    d. Summative assessments only at the end of a unit of study

42. A child understands object permanence and symbolism but is not yet able to form logical arguments. In which of Piaget's stages is this child?
    a. Sensorimotor
    b. Preoperational
    c. Concrete operational
    d. Formal operational

43. What is textual evidence?
    a. Passages from the book that the students are studying
    b. Information about the history or background of the text that the students are studying
    c. Clues that point to the meaning of a word in the text that the students are studying
    d. Clues that suggest that the text that the students are studying is reputable

44. A kindergarten student is having difficulty distinguishing the letters *b* and *d*. The teacher should do which of the following?
    a. Have the student use a think-aloud to verbalize the directions of the shapes used when writing each letter.
    b. Have the student identify the letters within grade-appropriate texts.
    c. Have the student write each letter five times.
    d. Have the student write a sentence in which all of the letters start with either *b* or *d*.

45. Which is the largest contributor to the development of students' written vocabulary?
    a. Reading
    b. Directed reading
    c. Direct teaching
    d. Modeling

46. Which choice of skills is NOT part of Bloom's Taxonomy?
    a. Remembering and understanding
    b. Applying and analyzing
    c. Listening and speaking
    d. Evaluating and creating

47. Which choice contains examples of Tier 3 vocabulary?
    a. Fairly common words like "beneficial" and "legible"
    b. Basic words like "car" and "run"
    c. Specialized words like "chloroplast" and "Peloponnesian War"
    d. Compound words like "bookcase" and "sunglasses"

48. A reader is distracted from following a story because he's having trouble understanding why a character has decided to cut school, so the reader jumps to the next page to find out where the character is headed. This is an example of what?
    a. Self-monitoring comprehension
    b. KWL charts
    c. Metacognitive skills
    d. Directed reading-thinking activities

49. What are the three interconnected indicators of reading fluency?
   a. Phonetics, word morphology, and listening comprehension
   b. Accuracy, rate, and prosody
   c. Syntax, semantics, and vocabulary
   d. Word exposure, phonetics, and decodable skills

50. What are the two types of vocabulary knowledge?
   a. Recognition and production
   b. Reliability and pronunciation
   c. Recognition and procedure
   d. Reliability and production

51. When gathering information from the internet, websites are more likely to provide factual, reliable information if the website domain ends with which of the following?
   a. .com
   b. .edu
   c. .org
   d. .net

52. A teacher needs to assess students' accuracy in reading high frequency sight words and irregular sight words that are grade-appropriate. Which of the following strategies would be most appropriate for this purpose?
   a. The teacher gives students a list of words to study for a spelling test that will be administered the following week.
   b. The teacher allows students to bring their favorite books from home and has them read their selected text aloud independently.
   c. The teacher administers the Stanford structural analysis assessment to determine students' rote memory and application of morphemes contained within the words.
   d. The teacher records how many words each student reads correctly when reading aloud a list of a teacher-selected, grade-appropriate words.

53. What is a readability formula?
   a. An equation for scoring how fast your students can read
   b. A method of making texts more predictable
   c. A way of calculating how long it will take to read a text
   d. A mathematical equation for calculating the difficulty of a test

54. Phonemic awareness, phonics, fluency, vocabulary, and comprehension are the five basic elements of what?
   a. Bloom's Taxonomy
   b. Spelling instruction
   c. Reading education
   d. Genre

55. Kimberly draws a picture of her family and then is asked by her instructor to write on the line below the picture what she drew. She puts together a jumble of letter-like forms rather than a series of discrete letters. The instructor asks her what she wrote and she replies, "My family." Which stage of spelling development is Kimberly in?
   a. Pre-phonetic stage
   b. Semiphonetic stage
   c. Phonetic stage
   d. Conventional stage

56. What is morphemic analysis?
   a. Guessing how to spell a word by thinking about its sounds
   b. Defining words by analyzing their parts
   c. Changing a word's meaning by adding a prefix
   d. Defining words by analyzing their sounds

57. If the majority of students in the classroom did not master a skill, what is the next step that a teacher should take?
   a. Reteach the skill to the entire class
   b. Break the class into smaller groups to remediate the skill
   c. Have students mediate with each other about the skill
   d. Move on to the next skill because time is critical

58. Samantha is in second grade and struggles with fluency. Which of the following strategies is likely to be most effective in improving Samantha's reading fluency?
   a. The teacher prompts Samantha when she pauses upon coming across an unknown word when reading aloud.
   b. The teacher records Samantha as she reads aloud.
   c. The teacher reads a passage out loud several times to Samantha and then has Samantha read the same passage.
   d. The teacher uses read-alouds and verbalizes contextual strategies that can be used to identify unfamiliar words.

59. A teacher notices that four students in a class of twenty are struggling to understand consonant phonics after a formal assessment. What course of action should the teacher take?
   a. Give the students a few days to study and have them retake the same assessment the following week
   b. Group the struggling students together and have them practice reading through the same words before reassessing
   c. Show a movie to the class and point out the consonant sounds used in various words
   d. Continue with planned lessons since only a small percentage of the overall group is behind

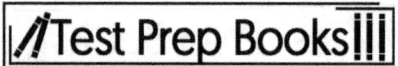

Practice Test

60. A child reads the story "Little Red Riding Hood" aloud. He easily pronounces the words, uses an apprehensive tone to show that the main character should not be leaving the path, adds a scary voice for the Big Bad Wolf, and reads the story at a pace that engages the class. What are these promising signs of?
   a. Reading fluency
   b. Phonemic awareness
   c. Reading comprehension
   d. Working memory

61. A teacher working with nonfiction texts may help students understand the difference between a main idea and a topic by explaining that the main idea is which of the following?
   a. The subject of the text
   b. The message to the reader
   c. The writer's thoughts on the topic
   d. A clear statement of the writer's stance

62. What do informal reading assessments allow that standardized reading assessments do NOT allow?
   a. The application of grade-level norms toward a student's reading proficiency
   b. The personalization of reading assessments in order to differentiate instruction based on the needs of individual students
   c. The avoidance of partialities in the interpretation of reading assessments
   d. The comparison of an individual's reading performance to that of other students in the class

63. A student is trying to decide if a character is telling the truth about having stolen candy. After the student reads that the character is playing with an empty candy wrapper in her pocket, the student decides the character is guilty. This is an example of what?
   a. Flashback
   b. Making inferences
   c. Style
   d. Figurative language

64. Which of the following is NOT an essential component of effective fluency instruction?
   a. Spelling
   b. Feedback
   c. Guidance
   d. Practice

65. If the entire class is struggling to understand the tone of voice used in a play, what is the best method for improving comprehension?
   a. Show the class a video of the play so that they can hear the tone being used and then have them act it out themselves
   b. Separate the class into small groups and have the students work on different aspects of the play, such as vocabulary, tone, and themes
   c. Have the students read through the play a few more times before taking an exam asking them to identify the tone in different parts
   d. Switch to a different reading principle before coming back to the subject of tone

144

66. A student is trying to read the word *preferred*. She first recognizes the word *red* at the end, then sounds out the rest of the word by breaking it down into "pre," then "fer," then "red." Finally she puts it together and says "preferred." This student is displaying what attribute?
   a. Phonemic awareness
   b. Phonics
   c. Fluency
   d. Vocabulary

67. What is the difference between a discussion circle and a debate?
   a. A discussion has no "right" or "wrong" side, whereas a debate does.
   b. A discussion is more formal than a debate.
   c. A debate breaks the students into two teams, whereas a discussion circle is a single group.
   d. A debate harms a student's sense of community, whereas a discussion builds community.

68. When selecting and organizing intervention groups, which of the following is most important?
   a. Organizing students according to their level
   b. Organizing students according to their grades on their prior report cards
   c. Organizing students according to the opinions of the students' previous teachers
   d. Organizing students according to their behavior in the classroom

69. Which elements do teachers count when they use Fry's formula?
   a. The chapters and pages in the whole book
   b. The number of paragraphs and sentences in three random sections
   c. The number of syllables and sentences in three 100-word passages
   d. The paragraphs and pages in the whole book

70. In the word *shut*, the *sh* is an example of what?
   a. Consonant digraph
   b. Sound segmentation
   c. Vowel digraph
   d. Rime

71. Which of the following is the most appropriate assessment of spelling for students who are performing at the pre-phonetic stage?
   a. Sight word drills
   b. Phonemic awareness tests
   c. Writing samples
   d. Concepts about print (CAP) test

72. Caregiver involvement is vital in reading initiatives. What can teachers do to foster this engagement?
   a. Assign independent reading for home.
   b. Invite caregivers to the class to read or talk about reading.
   c. Ask students about their access to books at home.
   d. Send books home for read-aloud activities.

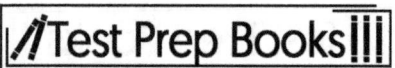

73. What is the role of a paraprofessional?
    a. To teach lessons independently
    b. To design the curriculum
    c. To work under the supervision of a teacher to manage class behavior and support student learning
    d. To tutor struggling children outside of class

74. Sandra wants to improve her students' reading comprehension by using guiding questions. Which step should she take?
    a. She should ask students questions about their interests so that she can choose an engaging text.
    b. She should give students a dedicated time to ask questions about the text.
    c. She should give students questions after they read the text.
    d. She should give students questions before they read the text.

75. An exam compares students' scores to national or state averages. What kind of assessment is this exam?
    a. Performance-based
    b. Criterion-referenced
    c. Norm-referenced
    d. Screening

76. While reading, a student is able to place themselves in the shoes of the main character and imagine how they feel. Which two strategies should a teacher consider introducing to capitalize on this stage of development?
    a. Uncomplicated stories and complicated words
    b. Multicultural literature and discussions
    c. Varied literature and scientific theories
    d. Multicultural literature and ethical issues

77. Jack teaches his students phonics, and he also gives them a list of sight words and encourages them to look at the pictures in their reader for clues about the content. Which approach to reading is Jack using?
    a. Interactive
    b. Top-down
    c. Phonemic
    d. Bottom-up

78. A first grader that is in a classroom's reading center appears to be frustrated. How can the teacher best help this student find a book that is at the appropriate reading level?
    a. Have the student do a five-finger test for vocabulary
    b. Pick a new book for the student
    c. Have the student try to figure it out on their own
    d. Have a peer read the book to the student

79. When students identify the phonemes in spoken words, they are practicing which of the following?
    a. Sound blending
    b. Substitution
    c. Rhyming
    d. Segmentation

80. A teacher divides information into manageable sections so that students do not feel overwhelmed. Which instructional method is this teacher implementing?
   a. Incremental education
   b. Breakdown technique
   c. Differentiated education
   d. Scaffolding

Answer Explanations

1. A: Graphic organizers are a method of integrating knowledge and ideas. A graphic organizer can be one of many different visual tools for connecting concepts to help students understand information.

2. B: Nursery rhymes are used in kindergarten to develop phoneme recognition. Rhyming words are often almost identical except for their beginning letter(s), so rhyming is a great strategy to implement during the analytic phase of phoneme development.

3. C: Good reading strategies are essential for all subject areas across the curriculum. In order to excel in science and social studies, there needs to be a good reading foundation—especially in nonfiction texts. The United States documents or science and social studies textbooks may all be used to teach nonfiction. Informational magazines may have good nonfictional material, but these need to be selected carefully to ensure that the reading is appropriately substantive. Basal readers are also good examples of nonfiction text.

4. C: The most common measurement of reading rate includes the oral contextual timed readings of students. During a timed reading, the number of errors made within a given amount of time is recorded. This data can be used to determine if a student's rate is improving and if the rate falls within the recommended range for his or her grade level.

5. D: Although the reading corner should be a restful and enjoyable place to encourage students to read independently, it does not enhance reading comprehension directly. Choices *A*, *B*, and *C* all encourage enhancement of reading comprehension. Giving students a chance to read independently allows them to choose books they enjoy, read at their own pace, and develop a lifelong enjoyment of reading.

6. B: Students should read a wide variety of literary and informational texts to prepare for college. Texts may extend across a wide variety of genres, timelines, and cultural works. Nonfiction, fiction, cultural pieces, and United States documents are all excellent examples of texts to use during reading instruction.

7. C: Decoding should be assessed in context in addition to isolation. During such assessments, the students read passages from reading-level appropriate texts aloud to the teacher so that the teacher is better able to analyze a student's approach to figuring out unknown words. Decoding should also be assessed in isolation. In these types of assessments, students are given a list of words and/or phonics patterns. Initially, high-frequency words that follow predictable phonics patterns are presented. The words that are presented become more challenging as a student masters less difficult words.

8. D: Print awareness includes all of the answer choices except the spelling of sight words. Print awareness includes Choice *A*, the differentiation of uppercase and lowercase letters, so that students can understand which words begin a sentence. Choice *B*, the identification of word boundaries, is also included in print awareness; that is, students should be made aware that words are made up of letters and that spaces appear between words, etc. Choice *C*, the proper tracking of words, is also included in print awareness, which is the realization that print is organized in a particular way, so books must be tracked and held accordingly.

9. B: Expository writing is detached and to the point, while other types of writing—persuasive, narrative, and argumentative—are lively. Since expository writing is designed to instruct or inform, it usually involves directions and steps written in second person ("you" voice) and lacks any persuasive or

Answer Explanations

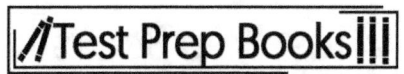

narrative elements. While argumentative writing is certainly to the point, it isn't detached because it includes the author's perspective and point of view.

10. C: An individual sound. A phoneme is the smallest unit of sound (for example, the phonogram "ph" represents the phoneme /f/). Choice *A*, a word, is typically composed of multiple phonemes. Choice *B* refers to phonics, and Choice *D* is a subtype of phoneme.

11. C: Advanced students can benefit from intervention groups by allowing the students to be challenged with more complex assignments. These assignments can be worked on independently and can include more difficult questions or higher-level vocabulary. Even short projects may be beneficial for these advanced students to work on throughout the week.

12. A: The identification of morphemes within words occurs during the instruction of structural analysis. Structural analysis is a word recognition skill that focuses on the meanings of word parts, or morphemes, during the introduction of a new word. Choice *B*, syllabic analysis, is a word analysis skill that helps students split words into syllables. Choice *C*, phonics, is the direct correspondence between and blending of letters and sounds. Choice *D*, the alphabetic principle, teaches that letters or other characters represent sounds.

13. C: Freytag's pyramid maps the events that contribute to the general structure of a story's plot. Choices *A* and *B* involve course planning, and Choice *D* describes characters, which are not part of Freytag's pyramid.

14. A: The rhythmic sounds and rhyming words of some poems help build a child's phonemic awareness.

15. A: A reading corner is not designed to be a "hang out" for students. Rather, it is a place for students to share thoughts on books or discuss recommendations. A reading corner should have a fun atmosphere to enhance students' interest in reading and be filled with a variety of genres and levels.

16. B: The student is performing at the phonetic stage. Phonetic spellers will spell a word as it sounds. The speller perceives and represents all of the phonemes in a word. However, because phonetic spellers have limited sight word vocabulary, irregular words are often spelled incorrectly.

17. B: Structural analysis focuses on the meaning of morphemes. Morphemes include base words, prefixes, and word endings (inflections and suffixes) that are found within longer words. Students can use structural analysis skill to find familiar word parts within an unfamiliar word in order to decode the word and determine the definition of the new word. The prefix im- (meaning not) in the word improbable can help students derive the definition of an event that is not likely to occur.

18. D: Students who struggle with comprehension may further be stymied by encountering words they are unfamiliar with in their readings. For those learners, providing a list of vocabulary words will improve their comprehension and help them build confidence in their reading abilities. Choice *A* is incorrect because vocabulary is focused on language knowledge rather than spelling. Choice *B* is incorrect. A vocabulary list will increase their familiarity with the meaning of the word and perhaps its recognition, but it will not speed up their reading if they are encountering it for the first time. Choice *C* is incorrect as well. Both groups of students will be required to use the dictionary for this assignment. Regardless of whether a student looks up the word before or after reading, the same dictionary skills will be required.

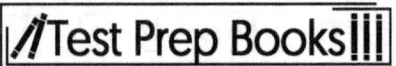

Answer Explanations

19. B: Flexibility is a central component of learner-centered education. Choice *A* is untrue because older materials may rely on outdated research. Choice *C* is false because combining two programs may allow teachers to benefit from the strengths of both methods. Choice *D* is not true because your coworkers are not necessarily using the best programs in their classes; talking to other teachers is a great idea, but you should take their advice with a grain of salt.

20. A: Fallacies are invalid logical processes. For example, consider the following argument: "Sam is an animal. He is not a cat, so he must be a dog." This is a fallacy because cats and dogs are not the only two animals. Choices *B* and *C* refer to the claim rather than the thought process. Choice *D* refers to criteria for evaluating sources.

21. A: Building a diverse classroom library, decorating the classroom, and integrating technology with her lessons will all contribute to students' ability to absorb information. Choice *B* excludes technology, which may be helpful to some students but harmful to others. Choice *C* is a minimalist approach, which goes against the information-rich principle of offering a variety of information and methods. Choice *D* also avoids decorations, which teach students and help them stay motivated.

22. D: Typographic features that help students locate key ideas or understand the structure of a piece of text are important when teaching reading comprehension.

23. C: Sight words are usually short, common words. Because it is not worth the effort to memorize words that will not appear frequently or are hard to distinguish from other words, sight words are words that are in frequent use and are short (for example, "so," "or," and "but"). Choice *A* is incorrect because phonics is usually taught before or at the same time as sight words. Choices *B* and *D* are not true because sight words were popular from the 1970s to the 1980s and are still used today.

24. B: Annotating texts teaches students to determine what information is important. Choices *A* and *C* may be true in some cases, but they are not necessarily related to annotation. Choice *D* is false because annotating does not involve class discussion.

25. B: Asking a paraprofessional to teach would be inappropriate because it asks them to work without the teacher's supervision and take full responsibility for the class. Choices *A*, *C*, and *D* are appropriate because they all occur under the teacher' supervision and do not place too much responsibility on the paraprofessional.

26. B: The role of a reading specialist is not to tell teachers how to do their jobs, but rather to assist them. One role of a reading coach is to help teachers in their classrooms with assessing students or even teach lessons for teachers. Another role of a reading specialist is to inform staff of district changes at staff meetings, in-services, or in professional development opportunities. Such changes may include alterations of curriculum or state standards.

27. C: The best way to encourage independent word learning and help students expand their vocabularies is by teaching them to use a dictionary. Pre-teaching words involves the teacher, and pairing up for reading involves other students, so neither are independent learning strategies. Assigning extra essays is an independent activity that will make students to write more, but that doesn't mean that they will use new words to do so.

28. B: Since diagnostic assessments focus on specific skills, they meet Laura's needs best. A screening assessment, Choice *A*, screens for at-risk students instead of providing a more detailed assessment. A

150

Answer Explanations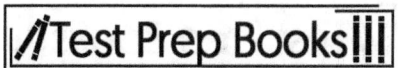

progress monitoring assessment, Choice C, is administered several times a year to track student progress, not at the first to identify areas of struggle. Outcomes assessments, Choice D, typically occur at the end of the year and are used to assess final understanding rather than diagnose concerns.

29. A: Phonological awareness is best assessed through identification of rimes or onsets within words. Instruction of phonological awareness includes detecting and identifying word boundaries, syllables, onset/rime, and rhyming words.

30. C: By definition, morphology is the identification and use of morphemes such as root words and affixes. Listening comprehension refers to the processes involved in understanding spoken language. Word consciousness refers to the knowledge required for students to learn and effectively utilize language. Textual analysis is an approach that researchers use to gain information and describe the characteristics of a recorded or visual message.

31. D: The instructional level is composed of 70 to 85% comprehension. Choice A requires 90 to 100% accuracy. Choice B measures students' auditory comprehension, so it is not relevant in this case. Choice C refers to comprehension below 70%.

32. C: Early learning should include vocabulary; however, by the time students progress to the writing process, they should have the vocabulary they need to express their ideas. In addition, the writing process is about organization and ideas more than words themselves. Feedback, Choice A, is vital to the teaching of writing. Students must, on a first draft, see not only corrections of grammar and punctuation or sentence structure but also ensure that their ideas are fully developed and their points supported rather than just listing point after point. Revision, Choice B, is essential for a student to apply the instruction and direction provided in a teacher's feedback. Finally, in order for a student to gather their thoughts, they must engage in a prewriting activity, Choice D, to determine their topic, their ideas, and how they may wish to communicate them.

33. C: Discussion circles focus specifically on ideas, topics, or issues that may arise in a text, but this method allows students to connect them to their own lives or experiences. As a result, the discussions are less focused on the text and more focused on complex and/or abstract ideas students must explore deeply. Choice A is incorrect because a literature circle focuses on the text students have read so they may focus more on details, plot, and characters rather than delving too deeply into complex ideas. Choice B is incorrect; jigsaw discussions involve students who have not read the same text. Therefore, in the final conversation, students must convey information they have read to students who have not read the same material, so the conversations do not get that in-depth. They are synthesizing information. Choice D is incorrect because there is limited discussion in role-play. Instead, students are acting out what they have read in a text, and therefore in-depth discovery and exploration is unlikely.

34. A: The alphabetical principle is the understanding that letters represent sounds in words. It is through the alphabetic principle that students learn the interrelationships between letter-sound (grapheme-phoneme) correspondences, phonemic awareness, and early decoding skills (such as sounding out and blending letter sounds).

35. D: Teachers should capitalize on the transfer of relevant skills from the learner's original language(s). In this way, extra attention and instructional emphasis can be applied toward the teaching of sounds and meanings of words that are nontransferable between the two languages.

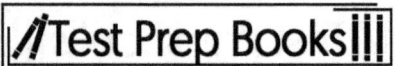

Answer Explanations

36. A: The Newberry Medal is annually offered to books for young readers. Choices *B* and *C* are not awards that are offered to children's books.

37. C: Jasmine needs to assess the students first so that she knows which areas of the program need improvement. She can then modify the program, test her modifications, and reassess her students to see whether these modifications have been successful. Choice *A* cannot be true because modifying the program before identifying its weaknesses would be pointless. Choice *B* has the same problem, and it adds the mistake of reassessing students before experimenting with different techniques. Finally, Choice *D* adds another mistake by placing experimentation before the initial assessment.

38. A: "Text evidence" refers to taking phrases and sentences directly from the text and writing them in the answer. Students are not asked to paraphrase, nor use any other resources to address the answer. Therefore, Choices *B*, *C*, and *D* are incorrect.

39. A: Voice is the primary trait that shows the individual writing style of an author. It is based on an author's choice of common syntax, diction, punctuation, character development, dialogue, etc.

40. C: Phonics allows readers to effectively translate print into recognizable speech. If children lack proficiency in phonics, their ability to read fluently and to increase vocabulary will be limited.

41. A: Assessments should always be frequent and ongoing for all students, but especially for those with special needs. These assessments may be informal but given daily after direct instruction and modeling. Summative assessments are important, but this should not be the first and only assessment during a unit of study, as these types of assessments are given at the end of a unit of study. Weekly and monthly assessments are not frequent enough for instructors to identify struggling areas and for successful remediation and intervention.

42. B: Preoperational. Piaget's stages are the sensorimotor stage (birth to two years), the preoperational stage (two to seven years), the concrete operational stage (seven to eleven years), and the formal operational stage (eleven years and older). Children learn symbolism in the preoperational stage, and they have already learned object permanence in the sensorimotor stage. However, they will not learn how to use logic correctly until the concrete operational stage. The answer cannot be Choice *A* because sensorimotor children do not understand object permanence and symbolism. It cannot be Choice *C* or Choice *D* because children in the concrete and formal operational stages would know how to form logical arguments.

43. A: Textual evidence comes from the primary text, the one that the students are studying. Choice *B* is wrong because it comes from secondary sources. Choice *C* refers to contextual clues, and Choice *D* refers to criteria for assessing research.

44. A: The teacher should have the student use a think-aloud to verbalize the directions of the shapes used when writing each letter. During think-alouds, teachers voice the metacognitive process that occurs when writing each part of a given letter. Students should be encouraged to do likewise when practicing writing the letters.

45. A: There is a positive correlation between a student's exposure to text and the academic achievement of that individual. Therefore, students should be given ample opportunities to read as much text as possible independently in order to gain vocabulary and background knowledge.

Answer Explanations

46. C: Listening and speaking are not part of Bloom's Taxonomy. The six parts are remembering, understanding, applying, analyzing, evaluating, and creating.

47. C: Tier 3 is composed of uncommon words that are only used in specific contexts, such as "chloroplast" in biology and "Peloponnesian War" in history. Choice *A* is composed of Tier 1 words, and Choice *B* is made up of Tier 1 vocabulary. The types of words in Choice *D* can fall under Tier 1 or Tier 2 vocabulary.

48. A: Scanning future portions of the text for information that helps resolve a question is an example of self-monitoring. Self-monitoring takes advantage of students' natural ability to recognize when they understand the reading and when they do not. KWL charts are used to help guide students to identify what they already know about a given topic. Metacognitive skills are when learners think about their thinking. Directed reading-thinking activities are done before and after reading to improve critical thinking and reading comprehension skills.

49. B: Key indicators of reading fluency include accuracy, rate, and prosody. Phonetics and decodable skills aid fluency. Syntax, semantics, word morphology, listening comprehension, and word exposure aid vocabulary development.

50. A: Recognition is knowing what a word means, and production is being able to call it to mind. Choices *B*, *C*, and *D* all contain misnomers.

51. B: Website domains ending in *.edu* are educational sites and tend to offer more reliable research in their field. A *.org* ending tends to be used by nonprofit organizations and other community groups, which can sometimes offer reliable information, but they aren't as trustworthy as *.edu* sites. A *.com* domain ending indicates a privately-owned website, as does a *.net*. Websites affiliated with official organizations and institutes of learning are more likely to offer fact-checked, reliable information.

52. D: Accuracy is measured via the percentage of words that are read correctly with in a given text. Word-reading accuracy is often measured by counting the number of errors that occur per 100 words of oral reading. This information is used to select the appropriate level of text for an individual.

53. D: A readability formula estimates text complexity. Choices *A* and *C* are both incorrect because they focus on speed rather than complexity. Choice *B* refers to predictable structure, which is a feature of simple text, not a readability formula.

54. C: The five basic components of reading education are phonemic awareness, phonics, fluency, vocabulary, and comprehension.

55. A: Kimberly is in the pre-phonetic stage of spelling because she formed a jumble of letter-like forms rather than a series of discrete letters. This indicates she has precommunicative writing ability only. Her letter-sound correspondences is limited. In the semiphonetic stage, she would have demonstrated a better understanding of the fact that letters represent sounds. She might have missing syllables in her words or possibly just single letters to represent entire words, but letter formation and the alphabetic principle would be demonstrated. In the other choices, her spelling would be even further advanced.

56. B: Morphemes are the smallest units of meaning, and morphemic analysis is the process of breaking words into morphemes and using them to deduce the meaning of the word. Choices *A* and *D* refer to sounds, so they are related to phonemic rather than morphemic analysis. Choice *C* does mention a morpheme (the prefix), but it involves changing the word instead of analyzing it to determine meaning.

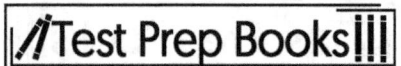

Answer Explanations

57. A: If the majority of the class did not master a skill taught, then the best plan is to reteach the skill to the entire class again. To break the class into intervention groups would not be the best use of time. Also, if many students did not understand the skill, then perhaps the skill was not properly taught the first time. A different teaching approach may need to be used. The utilization of different types of media, more direct instruction, and modeling of the skill should be done several more times before the students are assessed on the skill a second time.

58. D: This answer alludes to both read-alouds and think-alouds. Modeling fluency can be done through read-alouds. Proper pace, phrasing, and expression of text can be modeled when teachers read aloud to their students. During think-alouds, teachers verbalize their thought processes when orally reading a selection. Teachers' explanations may describe strategies they use as they read to monitor their comprehension. In this way, teachers explicitly model the metacognition processes that good readers use to construct meaning from a text.

59. B: Choice *B* is the correct answer. A small group of students is struggling with a specific principle. Therefore, the best course of action is to pivot toward small-group instruction. Giving the students an activity that they can work on together will encourage growth in the subject that they have difficulty with. They can then be reassessed to make sure that they have grasped the concept. Choice *A* is incorrect because reassessing the students without first providing differentiated instruction will not aid in their learning process. Choice *C* is incorrect because the group of students that are struggling is a small minority in the class, therefore it is unnecessary to go through a secondary whole-group lesson. Choice *D* is incorrect because the students who are struggling with that concept will need to grasp it before successfully continuing to lessons that build upon it.

60. A: If a child can accurately read text with consistent speed and appropriate expression while demonstrating comprehension, the child is said to have reading fluency skills. Without the ability to read fluently, a child's reading comprehension, Choice *C*, will be limited.

61. C: The main idea of a passage is the point the writer wants to make about the more general topic. The subject of the piece is the topic, so Choice *A* is incorrect. The message to the reader, Choice *B*, is the theme and is therefore incorrect. A thesis is a clear statement of the writer's stance, so Choice *D* is also incorrect.

62. B: Informal reading assessments allow teachers to create differentiated assessments that target reading skills of individual students. In this way, teachers can gain insight into a student's reading strengths and weaknesses. Informal assessments can help teachers decide what content and strategies need to be targeted. However, standardized reading assessments provide all students with the same structure to assess multiple skills at one time. Standardized reading assessments cannot be individualized. Such assessments are best used for gaining an overview of student reading abilities.

63. B: Making inferences is a method of deriving meaning that is intended by the author but not explicitly stated in the text. A flashback is a scene set earlier than the main story. Style is a general term for the way something is done. Figurative language is text that is not to be taken literally.

64. A: Practice is an essential component of effective fluency instruction. A student's accuracy and rate will likely increase if a teacher provides opportunities to learn words and use word-analysis skills. Oral reading accompanied by guidance and feedback from teachers, peers, or parents has a significant positive impact on fluency. In order to be beneficial, such feedback needs to target specific areas in which students need improvement, as well as strategies that students can use in order to improve in those areas. Such

Answer Explanations

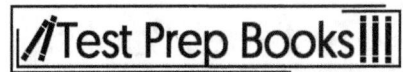

feedback increases students' awareness so that they can independently make needed modifications to improve fluency.

65. A: Choice *A* is the correct answer. Showing a video of the play and its actors will allow the students a different learning experience. They will be able to hear the tone being used and how it connects with the words of the play. Acting it out themselves will reinforce what they learned in an engaging way. Choice *B* is incorrect because small groups are unnecessary when the whole group is struggling with a concept. It is best to keep the students on the same page rather than breaking them up to learn different subjects. Choice *C* is incorrect because the students need further instruction before they can take another assessment. Choice *D* is incorrect because, since the whole group is struggling, it is appropriate to remain on the subject until it is complete. Switching subjects will only distance the students from what they have learned.

66. B: Phonics is the ability to apply letter-sound relationships and letter patterns in order to accurately pronounce written words. Phonemic awareness is the understanding that words are comprised of a combination of sounds. Fluency is an automatic recognition and accurate interpretation of text. Vocabulary is the body of words that a person knows.

67. C: Debates are built on two conflicting views, whereas discussion circles enable students to express their personal opinions; there might be as many opinions in the circle as there are students. Choice *A* is not necessarily true. Many issues and topics of morality, principles, ethics, and ideals are both discussed and debated, and there's often not a clear "right" or "wrong" side. Choice *B* is false because debates typically require more formal preparation than discussions. Choice *D* is untrue, as classroom debates can be a fun activity that also fosters a sense of community.

68. A: Intervention groups should be organized based on student performance. Although the behavior of students may be taken into consideration, the organization of group members should be primarily based on each student's performance level.

69. C: Fry's formula averages a book's word and sentence length to estimate complexity. Since Fry's formula demands three random sections and does not consider chapters, pages, or paragraphs, Choices *A*, *B*, and *D* are incorrect.

70. A: The sh is an example of a consonant digraph. Consonant diagraphs are combinations of two or three combinations of consonants that work together to make a single sound. Examples of consonant digraphs are sh, ch, and th. Choice *B*, sound segmentation, is used to identify component phonemes in a word, such as separating the /t/, /u/, and /b/ for tub. Choice *C*, vowel digraph, are sets of two vowels that make up a single sound, such as ow, ae, or ie. Choice *D*, rime, is the sound that follows a word's onset, such as the /at/ in cat.

71. C: Writing samples are the most appropriate assessment of spelling for students who are performing at the pre-phonetic stage. During the pre-phonetic stage, students participate in pre-communicative writing. Pre-communicative writing appears to be a jumble of letter-like forms rather than a series of discrete letters. Samples of students' pre-communicative writing can be used to assess their understanding of the alphabetic principle and their knowledge of letter-sound correspondences.

72. B: Not only does this show the caregiver what the classroom environment is like in regard to reading, it directly involves them in the activity, and that's the primary goal of engagement activities: participation. In addition, it may help them understand their students' needs in regard to reading

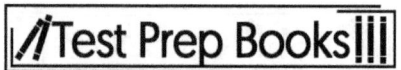

Answer Explanations

education. Choice *A* is incorrect; although reading at home is great for promoting a student's reading, it doesn't engage the caregiver. Choice *C* is incorrect; it might provide information about the reading culture at home, but it doesn't actively engage the caregiver. Finally, Choice *D* is incorrect. Although providing reading materials is a great tactic, it does not guarantee there will be engagement.

73. C: To work under the supervision of a teacher to manage class behavior and support student learning. Paraprofessionals help teachers, but do not hold the responsibility in the classroom. Choice *A* is untrue because paraprofessionals should not be working without teacher supervision. Choice *B* also places far too much responsibility on the paraprofessional. Choice *D* focuses on work outside the classroom, which is typically relegated to tutors rather than teaching aides.

74. D: Students look at guiding questions before they read a text, and they use the questions to identify important information in their reading. Choice *A* is a way to engage student interests, not offer comprehension support. Choice *B* involves the students asking the teacher questions, which is the opposite of the guiding question process. Choice *C* does involve reading comprehension, but it is a way of assessing rather than aiding understanding.

75. C: Because the test compares students' averages to averages from a wider population, it is norm-referenced. Choice *A* measures students' ability to apply concepts and is not used to compare students. Choice *B* compares students' skills to predetermined criteria instead of other students. Choice *D* is used to identify at-risk students. While some screening assessments may be norm-referenced, the exam described in the question must be norm-referenced.

76. B: In the concrete operational stage, students are developing empathy, so multicultural literature and discussions are great tools to continue to build on those skills. Although simple stories are great for early learners, complicated words should not be introduced until later, so Choice *A* is incorrect. Choices *C* and *D* are incorrect because scientific theories and ethical issues are not truly understood until the formal operational stage.

77. A: Interactive approach. The interactive approach means using elements of both the top-down and bottom-up approaches. In this question, Jack is using top-down methods by implementing phonics, and bottom-up methods by using sight words and guessing strategies. Because he is using both approaches in conjunction, he must be using the interactive approach. Choice *B* cannot be correct because it would only allow Jack to use sight words, and Choice *D* cannot be correct because it would allow only phonics. Choice *C* is a method within Choice *D*, so it is also not a viable option.

78. A: Young students should use the five-finger test to select an appropriate-level text. Using the five-finger test, a student selects a page within a text that he or she wants to read. The student holds up a finger for each word he or she is unable to read on that page. If the student has five fingers up after reading the entire page, then the student should stop and choose a book at an easier reading level. If there are not a variety of books of various reading levels from which a student can choose, then the student is likely to become frustrated. Such frustration may cause the student to stop reading for pleasure and see reading as a chore.

79. D: Phoneme segmentation is the identification of all the component phonemes in a word. An example would be the student identifying each separate sound, /t/, /u/, and /b/, in the word tub. Choice *A*, sound blending, is the blending together of two or more sounds in a word, such as /ch/ or /sh/. Choice *B*, substitution, occurs when a phoneme is substituted within a word for another phoneme, such as substituting the sound /b/ in bun to /r/ to create run. Choice *C*, rhyming, is an effective tool to utilize

156

Answer Explanations

during the analytic phase of phonics development because rhyming words are often identical except for their beginning letters.

80. D: Scaffolding is breaking material into chunks so that students can learn it more easily. Choices *A* and *B* are both misnomers for scaffolding. Choice *C* refers to giving students alternatives in education, not breaking down information.

Dear FTCE Test Taker,

Thank you for purchasing this study guide for your FCTE exam. We hope that we exceeded your expectations.

Our goal in creating this study guide was to cover all of the topics that you will see on the test. We also strove to make our practice questions as similar as possible to what you will encounter on test day. With that being said, if you found something that you feel was not up to your standards, please send us an email and let us know.

We have study guides in a wide variety of fields. If you're interested in one, try searching for it on Amazon or send us an email.

FTCE General Knowledge

This can be found on Amazon: amazon.com/dp/1637752873

FTCE Elementary Education

amazon.com/dp/1628457074

Thanks Again and Happy Testing!
Product Development Team
info@studyguideteam.com

FREE Test Taking Tips Video/DVD Offer

To better serve you, we created videos covering test taking tips that we want to give you for FREE. **These videos cover world-class tips that will help you succeed on your test.**

We just ask that you send us feedback about this product. Please let us know what you thought about it—whether good, bad, or indifferent.

To get your **FREE videos**, you can use the QR code below or email freevideos@studyguideteam.com with "Free Videos" in the subject line and the following information in the body of the email:

    a. The title of your product

    b. Your product rating on a scale of 1-5, with 5 being the highest

    c. Your feedback about the product

If you have any questions or concerns, please don't hesitate to contact us at info@studyguideteam.com.

Thank you!

www.ingramcontent.com/pod-product-compliance
Lightning Source LLC
Chambersburg PA
CBHW060514300426
44112CB00017B/2658